PRAISE FOR
Evangel**preneur**

"When I first met Josh and read the principles of *Evangelpreneur*, I thought to myself: 'The Kingdom of Heaven is *just like that!*' Chain-breaking, life-giving stuff."

—SR. PASTOR TROY BREWER,
Open Door Church

"Listening to you talk, Josh, I'm ready to do something! I'm ready to bust down some walls somewhere!"

—ANDY ALBRIGHT,
CEO of National Agents Alliance

"Congratulations, Josh. You hit the ball out of the park with your latest book, *Evangelpreneur*. This is a must-read for anyone who wants to have a practical, readable, step-by-step guide to becoming an 'Evangelpreneur.' I have read numerous self-help, motivational, and leadership-type books. Your approach is fresh as well as balanced. I am a better Christian, minister, citizen, provider, husband, father, and grandfather as a result of your book. I am in your debt."

—PASTOR MICHAEL JACKSON,
New Life Assembly of God

"Thoroughly impressed. Good job on your speaking and writing. Very rarely do you find someone who can do both well."

"The committed always conquer the complacent and Josh Tolley's valiant volume reveals how the rituals and restraints of religion build commitment. By boldly brandishing the banner of faith in the area of wealth creation, Josh describes the road map to real riches. This book contains valuable insights that will help the fiscal transformation of all readers."

"We have had the had the privilege to book *every* past president since Reagan and superstars like Michael Jordan, Payton Manning, Dr. Wayne Dyer, and Jack Canfield. Josh Tolley is one of the best speakers I have ever witnessed. Josh is the BEST!"

"Go into any Christian bookstore and you'll find a plethora of books that teach you how to 'name it and claim it' or achieve vast riches with some secret Biblical principle. This book isn't one of those. Josh Tolley has provided a concise program for handling finances by changing how one thinks about money and labor, while remaining in fidelity to Biblical ethics and morals. This book does not fill the reader with outlandish claims of financial prosperity just because one prays for it, but details the steps one needs to take in order to achieve financial success that is within everyone's grasp. Tolley has provided reasoned, logical, proven and, most important, Biblically consistent approaches to good stewardship. If you're serious about being that good steward, you need this book!"

—FR. JACK ASHCRAFT,
featured on The Travel Channel and Animal Planet

"I believe every Christian needs to read this book! Josh's book teaches us how to implement the following two verses in our lives:

Deuteronomy 28:13 *'And the Lord shall make thee the head, and not the tail; and thou shalt be above only, and not beneath...'* Deuteronomy 8:18 *'But thou shalt remember the LORD thy God: for it is He that giveth thee power to get wealth, that He may establish His covenant which He sware unto thy fathers, as it is this day.'"*

—PASTOR RICK RYAN,
Arizona Bible Church

"Wow! How I wish I had this book when I started out decades ago. As a successful businessman and Christian, this power-house of financial management would have saved me tons of time and money during some of my terribly uninformed trial and error years! In *Evangelpreneur*, those principles are available to all through practical, uncompromising, unrelentingly motivational common sense and Scriptural dissertation."

—DR. THOMAS R. HORN,
author of Blood on the Altar *and founder of SkyWatch TV*

"Josh nails it in *Evangelpreneur*...You will truly be empowered once you know the truth about money and its relationship to a fulfilled and Godly life."

—TERRY WHIPPLE,
cofounder of iLead Entrepreneurial Charter Schools

"As Josh Tolley brings up in his brand new powerful book on finances—the Bible talks about providing financially for yourself, your children, and your children's children, but with majority of Americans just one paycheck (or less) away from the poverty line! Is it ever God's will for someone not to be able to provide for their offspring? The Bible calls poverty a curse, so are four out of five churchgoers cursed?

This is a book that incorporates all of the Scriptures, including our responsibilities when it comes to money, the solid Biblical principles to follow, and the concept of free enterprise. This book challenges us all to look into what we TRULY feel about money! How to get free to use our money wisely to provide for our family and for our ministry! How to have provision for fulfilling the destiny and purpose that God has entrusted us to achieve while we are on planet earth.

I highly recommend this book as it is unlike any book you'll ever read to help us in our endeavors to be Godly men and women showing forth the kingdom of the most high God."

—WARREN MARCUS,
vice president of TV, Radio, and Development
for Sid Roth's It's Supernatural

HOW BIBLICAL
FREE ENTERPRISE
CAN EMPOWER YOUR FAITH,
FAMILY, AND FREEDOM

REVISED AND EXPANDED EDTION

Josh Tolley

BenBella Books, Inc.
Dallas, TX

BenBella Books, Inc.
10440 N. Central Expressway
Suite #800
Dallas, TX 75231
www.benbellabooks.com
Send feedback to feedback@benbellabooks.com

BenBella is a federally registered trademark.

Printed in the United States of America
10 9 8 7 6 5 4 3 2 1

ISBN 978-1-637741-08-5

The Library of Congress has cataloged an earlier edition as follows:

Tolley, Josh.
  Evangelpreneur : how biblical free enterprise can empower your faith, family, and freedom / Josh Tolley.
    pages cm
  Includes bibliographical references and index.
  ISBN 978-1-940363-77-6 (paperback)—ISBN 978-1-940363-87-5 (electronic) 1. Economics—Religious aspects—Christianity. 2. Entrepreneurship—Religious aspects—Christianity. 3. Free enterprise—Religious aspects—Christianity.
I. Title.
  BR115.E3T595 2015
  261.8'5—dc23
                                                                  2014041350

Copyediting by James Fraleigh
Proofreading by Cape Cod Compositors, Inc. and Jordynn Prado
Cover design by Jason Gabbert
Cover photography by Spencer Avinger
Text design and composition by John Reinhardt Book Design
Printed by Lake Book Manufacturing

Special discounts for bulk sales are available.
Please contact bulkorders@benbellabooks.com.

This book is dedicated to you, the reader,
for it is you for whom I wrote this book.

May you continue to be brave enough to seek Truth
and the solutions that come with it!

Contents

Foreword

AM DELIGHTED AT HOW GOD has used, and is using, Josh Tolley as a champion for the free-enterprise system and the American dream of owning your own business. His book, *Evangelpreneur*, boldly exhorts people to return to the idea of personal responsibility and financial freedom.

I first connected with Josh Tolley about fifteen years ago at a coffee-shop business meeting. At that time he was twenty years old and embarking on his entrepreneurial education in *the school of hard knocks*.

I had already gotten my degree in that school, having owned over a dozen businesses by the time I was twenty-eight. My wife, Linda, reminds me how in the early years of our marriage I would wake up regularly at three in the morning with a new idea for a business. She called it "the idea of the month." Yet at twenty-eight, we were still broke. But I never gave up on that dream. By age thirty-two we were millionaires, and it's been uphill since then.

I grew up in an entrepreneurial family, my father being a self-employed millionaire. At a very early age I had a paper route and lawn-mowing business. At age twelve I got interested in the stock market, and began tracking and charting the price cycles of stocks. My father told our stockbroker to allow me to trade without his permission, and I began to invest my paper route money, growing it into a nice little nest egg.

Growing up in a Beverly Hills–type suburb, all my friends were given new cars by their parents when they turned sixteen. I remember going to my father on my sixteenth birthday and asking, "Dad, when do I get my car?" He replied, "If you want a car, work for it."

The hard reality of *personal responsibility* was established.

Over the next twelve years I would work in a job long enough to save money to start my own business. I understood that all business is, is identifying a need and coming up with a solution to meet that need with a product or service.

The longest I ever worked for someone else was six months. I never was fired. I just quit. I would get bored. Every time I had a job I would look at the people around me, many of whom had been there fifteen to twenty years, and I would think, *Is this it? Is this all there is to life, just nine-to-five-ing it day after day, month after month, year after year?*

There has to be more to life than this, I concluded. Henry David Thoreau wrote, "The mass of men lead lives of quiet desperation," and that's how I felt every time I had a job.

Through his own enterprise, J. Paul Getty became the wealthiest man in the world, having tapped Saudi Arabia's oil riches to build one of the most successful petroleum companies in the world. In his book, *How to Be Rich,* he teaches that the number-one principle of financial success is that you've got to be in business for yourself.

Robert Kiyosaki, in his best-selling book *Rich Dad, Poor Dad,* explains this concept through the grid of the cash-flow quadrant. The "E quadrant" is the "Employment quadrant." This is where most people find themselves, working for someone else's dream. And your employer will pay you as little as he has to pay you to replace you. If he doesn't make a profit on your labor, he's out of business. Why then do people choose the E quadrant? The most common response I get is "job security."

As I went through my school of hard knocks with a myriad of unsuccessful businesses, my wife would continually implore me, "Can't you just get a secure job with a secure paycheck?" (She was being a good mother, wanting to make sure her baby chicks were taken care of.)

"Job security" is an oxymoron. We should more accurately call it "job insecurity." When someone has the ability to sign or not sign your paycheck, that's not secure. Your only security is in your ability to produce.

In 1900, 50 percent of Americans were self-employed. By 2013 that number had dropped to 6.6 percent. A July 2014 Harris poll found that only 39 percent of Americans had the hope of one day owning their own business. What in the world happened to the American dream of entrepreneurship and financial freedom?

In *Evangelpreneur*, Josh writes from his own experience of business ownership, encouraging people to return to their God-given right to free enterprise in a business of their own. In addition to being an entrepreneur himself, Josh has written and taught on the subject extensively, and owns and hosts a syndicated talk-radio show on the subject that is broadcast to millions of listeners in all fifty states and 160 countries. His program has interviewed some of the most successful entrepreneurs in the country, promulgating many of the principles he writes about in this book.

I reconnected with Josh as he interviewed me several months ago on his show. We immediately saw that we were like-minded on many levels.

For one, Josh and I are both committed Christians. The word "Christian" is used three times in the New Testament. In the original Greek text it means "Christ follower." So as best we can, Josh and I are committed to living 100 percent for Jesus and 0 percent for ourselves. The grid through which we see all of life is a Biblical grid, the Bible in our opinion being the Holy Spirit–inspired word of God.

Interestingly, a full 15 percent of the Bible is on money and possessions; there are 2,350 verses on the subject in Scripture. And since Josh and I view Scripture as God's operating manual on planet earth, we believe we need to go back to this Biblical teaching. I wrote a best-selling book on the subject some years ago titled *The Legend of the Monk and the Merchant*. In it, I teach Biblical financial principles in the context of a historical storyline that takes place in Venice and Rome in the 1500s. Dave Ramsey wrote the foreword to the book, and the last sixty pages contain a twelve-session Biblical study on marketplace ministry and money. This was the book Josh was interviewing me about on his radio show when we reconnected.

As Christians, Josh and I are aware of several things to which God has jointly called us. As we enjoy financial success ourselves, and as we teach others Biblical principles on success, we recognize that this is *prosperity with a purpose*. It's all about pointing people to our Lord. Psalm 37:4 says, "Delight thyself also in the Lord: and he shall give thee the desires of thine heart." My Jewish friends, who are more fluent in Hebrew than I am, tell me that this is mistranslated. It should read, "Delight yourself also in the Lord, and you will fulfill the desires of His heart." In other words, if you put God first, if He's your Lord and you're his bondservant (Romans 1, Philippians 1, James 1), then as best you can, you will be an imitator of Christ (1 Corinthians 11:1). And Jesus said in John 5:19 that the Son can do nothing of himself, but "what He seeth the Father do." As imitators of Christ, then, that should be our cry—that we can only do what the Holy Spirit leads us to do. In other words, as Christians it's not about us, it's about advancing His Kingdom (Matthew 28:18–20) and pointing people to Him.

So this is what Josh is all about, and this is what I'm all about.

And that's why I am excited to endorse and promote *Evangelpreneur*. It will challenge you—but that's a good thing. I believe we need to continually reassess our lives and our Christian walk. It's called *being continually transformed by the renewing of our minds*. So be blessed as these words bring revelation and life to you.

TERRY FELBER
Entrepreneur, Pastor, and
Author of *The Legend of the Monk and the Merchant*

Introduction

This Is Not Your Daddy's "Best Life Now" Book

ET'S START by cutting through the fog. There are literally thousands of books in the "faith" market that promise you your best life now, or say that prosperity is as easy as tying your shoes and that you have nothing to worry about—you can just name it and claim it. Here is a dose of harsh reality for you: Most people reading this book have less than $3,000 in the bank and are less than six months away from poverty if they were to lose their job.[1] As of late 2019, 59 percent of Americans were one paycheck away from homelessness.[2] These stats apply to the faithful, too, with research showing that 71 percent of Christians have debt beyond their mortgage, 97 percent know someone in their church who lost a job in the past twelve months, 66 percent of Christian households are experiencing negative or no increase financially, and 40 percent of Christians overspend their monthly income.[3] Chances are, one of these scenarios describes you.

Four out of five people in the United States of America are either below, at, or one paycheck away from the poverty level.[4] How can this be if you have been a person of faith for years? How can this be if you have read all the books and watched all the great pastors on television telling you that riches on earth are yours if you truly believe?

If those sobering statistics were not enough of a reality check, try this on for size: Churches are head over heels in debt, too. Foreclosure rates on *churches* are the highest they have ever been.[5] And the statistics don't even tell the whole truth. As I mentioned on my nationally syndicated talk show, those in the lending industry say it's actually much worse than what's reported, because "no bank wants to look like the bad guy and repo a church."[6]

How can this be? Churches teach us not to be a debtor (or a lender), so how can a church possibly owe money?

Given many churches' inability to pay their mortgages, it should come as no surprise that tithing is also at record lows.[7] I ask again as we start this book: How can this be? Isn't tithing one of the first commands in regard to money? The book of Malachi says not to tithe is to rob God (see the FAQ section for more information on Tithing).[8]

It comes down to this: The modern Church has so perverted the Biblical teachings in regard to money—what it's for, how to make it, and how to use it—that this wrong doctrine is rotting the Church body from the inside out. Some churches (and even some members themselves) are even dying because of it. To address this catastrophic problem we are now experiencing because of a lack of money and its proper use, those in charge of leading the Church body have embraced, in their ignorance, two approaches.

The first is to essentially say that God is in control, all things work to His glory, and money should not be a focus of instruction. If He decides to bless someone with money, it is His will. If not, it may be that He is strengthening that person. The second is a drastic opposite, with a preference toward claiming that just belief ("you gotta have faith") or the act of giving ("you reap what you sow") will be enough to open up the floodgates of Heaven. So ridiculous is the second approach that some teachers of this perversion have gone as far as offering special handkerchiefs that, if purchased at a nominal fee, will bring prosperity your way. If you purchased one of these handkerchiefs, I have some oceanfront property in Nebraska to sell you.

The danger with both of these approaches is that they are laced with just enough truth to make followers believe them. Yes, you need to have faith and God does bless our giving, but these are part of larger principles. While God does assist in our lives at times in a supernatural way, I believe He prefers to work in our lives through our reasoned and practical application of sound practices that He has empowered us to seek and understand. For example, He made the Israelites walk when He could have just moved the whole lot as He did with Philip in Acts 8. Again, we see in Yeshua (aka Jesus; see FAQ) providing a supernatural catch for His doubting disciples, yet they still have to fish and feed themselves again—it is not as if He supernaturally filled every need on a daily basis. He says in 2 Thessalonians 3:10, "For even when we were with you this we commanded you, that if any would not work, neither should he eat"; and throughout Scripture He gives practices for sound sowing and reaping, solid building, and good business dealings. It is clear that while His supernatural hand is at work, so, too, is His expectation that you should work in such a way that produces the best results possible. He actually goes so far as to point out that doing work in an unwise way is something that He punishes.

I remember being in a church, and as a guest speaker I was sitting up front. The pastor put out a call for those who needed prayer and a handful of people came forward. Sitting close enough to hear, I noted that as the pastor went from person to person, asking what they needed prayer about, all but one of the requests were financial.

For less than $20,000, those prayers, save one medical problem, could have been answered. It stands out as a powerful moment in my life. It was then that I started to realize that if the Church as a whole in this country and around the world is going to grow spiritually and in number, it needs to get back to proper teaching regarding money. Were those people seeking prayer not faithful? Did God really want that family to have a broken car? Did God lie when He said He would provide? Were we, as believers, asking too much and missing the fact that God was providing for us already? After all, He has sustained our lives, so in a deeper sense, He is indeed providing for us. Perhaps wanting our kids in clothes that fit is just greedy?

The Bible talks about providing *financially* for yourself, your children, and your children's children, but with the majority of Americans just one paycheck (or less) away from the poverty line, clearly this isn't happening in most homes. Is it ever God's will for someone *not* to be able to provide for their offspring? The Bible calls poverty a curse more than a hundred times, so are four out of five churchgoers cursed?

With these questions in mind, and thinking that there must be sound teachings on faith and finances, I went searching at a bookstore. To my disbelief, everything I found there fell into the two previous approaches (either that God is in control and blesses who He will, or the prosperity gospel). When I spoke to the management of this particular store about the lack of books addressing people's most common earthly problem, money, the response was, "No, unfortunately there is not really much out there. If someone were to come along with a book teaching the proper perspective on faith, finances, and business, we wouldn't be able to keep it on the shelves."

Of course, I thought the lack of credible information available at this store had to be a fluke. Perhaps the people who manage these retail outlets focusing on the faith demographic were atheists in disguise who didn't really care to see what was available to offer their customers. I decided to approach a few pastors and ask to speak with them regarding my views on faith and money. I spent a few hours providing my perspective of money and Biblical teaching, discussed what they were taught in their training, and answered several of their questions. Those conversations made it clear that the faithful need to reexamine their approach to finances, and how they should be walking in their daily lives. It was clear that there needed to be a book with a third approach, one that incorporated all of the Scriptures, including our responsibilities when it comes to money, the solid Biblical principles to follow, and the concept of free enterprise. You hold in your hands such a book.

Now, I would like to make it clear that I am not a professional theologian, nor am I a pastor. I do, however, have a Bible and a relationship with the Father. The financial insights I'm presenting here are from what I see in Scripture. In *Evangelpreneur* I will answer the questions people of faith have, yet have been taught not to ask—but we need to start asking them. It is time to be honest with ourselves and admit that there has been a lack of teaching and, in some cases, perverted teaching regarding money. This has left the faithful in a position that in many cases is worse than that of our secular friends when it comes to finances. How can we expect a world in pain to listen to the faithful if we are suffering just as much or more pain than those outside of the Church?

Before we start, I want to thank the brave congregations, leaders, and members who allowed me into their churches, temples, and synagogues to address this ignored topic. It encourages me to see so many people from so many denominations starting to recognize the problem and having the courage to help millions by helping me. You are not alone; you are not the only one facing this problem.

Getting out of debt is not nearly enough to bring us financial peace.

When this book first came out, I could never have imagined the impact that it has now had. It has become a three-time #1 bestseller on Amazon and a bestseller internationally, and has launched thousands of people into the life of an Evangelpreneur.

Hearing that people have returned to God in their Christian, Jewish, and even Islamic faith because of what they read and implemented from this book has been amazing. The marriages and families repaired, as well as the churches, temples, and synagogues no longer worried about every penny, bring a smile to my face daily.

Since the COVID-19 crisis, the relevance of this book, as well as the importance of the capital protection services we offer, has never been greater. The COVID crisis not only proved the first edition of this book to be correct but also woke people up economically like they haven't been in generations. The world has forever changed and in some ways we will not realize just how much for years to come. As the world recovers from the crisis, people are no longer looking towards banks and Wall Street to keep and protect their money. The illusion that employment provides any real security has been invalidated.

I've been teaching the principles in this book for decades, and while part of me would love to shout *I told you so* from the rooftops, the reality is that the consequences of not acting on the advice in this book are too dire for me to gloat. Now, more than ever, we need to have Evangelpreneurship as part of every family, every community, and every congregation.

A caveat: What we are going to be covering may be controversial and may challenge preconceived beliefs. We are going to examine together how getting out of debt is not nearly enough to bring us financial peace. We will also discover that our approach to employment, entrepreneurship, and money as a whole has actually made living out our faith harder to do. There may even be times when this book is painful to read. But I urge you to finish the book. I ask that you use your God-given mind and prayer to evaluate what is being taught. If, after reading the book, you still think the way you have been addressing faith and finances to this point is the way you need to continue, then by all means do so. For the rest of you, what you will take away from this book can very well change the world.

"Come now, and let us reason together"
—Isaiah 1:18

PART 1

Why Be an Evangelpreneur?

A Church of Believers in Bondage

How the Shackles of Debt Render Us Captive

ET US IMAGINE for a second that the world is about to end. Perhaps a series of nuclear bombs are on the brink of going off, maybe a meteor is set to hit the earth, or there's some other catastrophe. Then there is you, the man or woman who can save the day. You could disarm the bomb, or you may have the launch codes to the missile that would take out the meteor.

You are the hero because you are trained in Special Forces tactics, well versed in dynamic nuclear systems operation, or have advanced degrees in physics and astronomy. When emergencies like this arise, you are the one everyone looks to for rescue. Bottom line, you are fully aware of the situation and you are fully trained and capable of doing what is needed to stop the impending doom.

With that being the case, the world will be saved, right?

Not so fast. Let's add one more relevant piece of information to this story. Last night you decided to go out drinking and got a bit too pushy with a bouncer named Tiny. As dawn breaks the darkness of night, you wake up, only to find yourself shackled to a bed inside a steel cage at the county jail.

As you sit there fighting back the headache, you also fight back a sinking feeling, as through your cell you see on television this impending disaster you are fully equipped to prevent. Nobody else is coming to save the day, as it was you who fate had determined would answer the call. Yet here you find yourself stuck—and the worst part is, by your own doing.

Would you yell to the guards that you knew you could prevent the disaster if they would just let you out? Would you really expect them to believe you? Worse yet, could that kind of talk land you in a Department of Homeland Security detention center under the Patriot Act since your talk seems a bit too "alarmist"?

Would you fight the chains that bind you? Would you inform the others held in captivity with you in an effort to rally an escape attempt? Would you feel guilty about having done the wrong thing by getting locked up, which now places you in a position where you are unable to do the right thing? More importantly, would you actually be guilty of the world's destruction?

We cannot do the work God has called us to do because we are not operating financially in line with Biblical principles.

As thankful as many of us would be for not being placed in such a predicament, we still find ourselves in a dire situation. Unfortunately, the bad news is that our current situation is eerily close to the one I just described. Because debt is so prevalent in our lives, our financial situation, along with that of our nation and the Church as a whole, is in bondage. We cannot do the work God has called us to do because we are not operating financially in line with Biblical principles. We are over our heads in debt and not making enough to thrive, not to mention we are losing the battle against inflation—all of which is affecting our mission and effectiveness as believers.

Would you like to be the hero in this story who's not stuck in jail, but who is out doing the work God has called you to? Being an Evangelpreneur is the way to do this. What is an Evangelpreneur? An Evangelpreneur is someone who lives his or her life with the focus of spreading God's kingdom and will through the empowerment

He created in free enterprise. He or she uses the natural and supernatural to control the use of time and money to effectively live out the calling placed on his or her life.

This book will look at why I believe being an Evangelpreneur is God's purpose for believers and how we start down that path. However, before we can become an Evangelpreneur, we need to get a handle on debt. And to get a handle on debt, we need to see just how much it's crippling us, how it truly is keeping us in jail and from our rescue mission, just like the hero in the story.

Churches in Foreclosure

In 2010, Crystal Cathedral Ministries, which built one of the nation's largest and most famous churches, filed for bankruptcy. I have never thought of money as the most important thing in life, but the news of the church's financial collapse kind of shook me. Here, a church with thousands of members on location, and tens of thousands more watching on television around the world, had just gone bankrupt. My initial response was, "There must be more to this story." Perhaps a board member was embezzling funds, a pastor abusing the tithes and offerings, or even a robbery. As I waited for further information to come out, I kept telling myself that this must be a mistake. Certainly a ministry that brought in tens of millions of dollars *a year* would have no reason to declare bankruptcy unless there was some case of abuse or misuse. As a man born into sin myself, I know that an individual will have moments in life where they fall short. So I was sure that a scandalous revelation was going to be appearing on the nightly news any day now.

I waited and waited, but no story appeared. The truth was not only harder to believe than a scandal, but in a way, worse: The Crystal Cathedral couldn't pay its bills.

How could this be?

I remember thinking this would be easier to accept as true if there had been a misdeed by someone connected to the church. As bad and as scandalous as that would have been, I might have been more understanding. I had never been a donor of the Crystal Cathedral, but that really isn't the point. The point is, here was a major house of worship collapsing before a national audience, and it was all because the church was broke.

Keep in mind that we are talking not about an individual, but rather a church: a group of believers coming together to worship, instruct, and grow in their faith. This means there is a poor-leadership aspect to consider as well. To those who attended the Crystal Cathedral, either in person or via television, their church placed the needs of the people and the calling given in the Bible on the back burner in favor of worldly financial desires. The church is now sold and has become property of the local Catholic diocese, which has renamed it "Christ Cathedral" and will use it as a place of worship. Those who counted on the Crystal Cathedral are now left in the proverbial cold because the debt gamble (yes, it was a gamble) did not work out.

When a church has debt, including a mortgage, it is usually not just one person who made the error but rather a board of people who are mature in their faith, who all have to sign off on placing themselves and their church (including all other members) in bondage—I mean debt.

To the reader who does not have a belief system based on the Elohim of Abraham, Isaac, and Jacob, you may be asking yourself, "Why does this matter? What's the big deal if a church has a mortgage and debt?" The question is a great one from the perspective of a person outside of that belief system, but to someone who does have faith in the Author of the Bible, that Author clearly states, "For which of you, intending to build a tower, sitteth not down first, and counteth the cost, whether he have sufficient to finish it?" in Luke 14:28, *and* "The rich ruleth over the poor, and the borrower is servant to the lender" in Proverbs 22:7.

My response to learning of this gross mismanagement of funds and poor stewardship as it relates to the Crystal Cathedral left me thinking what I hope you are thinking, that certainly this is a one-case situation. Surely there are not many churches in this predicament.

Then I started doing some research.

It turns out that the bankruptcy of the Crystal Cathedral is not an anomaly at all. In fact, I learned that the Western world is facing record numbers of church foreclosures!

As I mentioned in the Introduction, church foreclosures are at an all-time high, according to CoStar, and individuals in the lending industry say that this crisis may be even worse than what those official foreclosure statistics suggest, because nobody wants to look like the bad guy and go after a church.

This was confirmed by Scott Rolfs, managing director of religious and education finance at Ziegler, an investment bank, in an article on the *Huffington Post*. "Churches are among the final institutions to get foreclosed upon because banks have not wanted to look like they are being heavy handed with the churches," said Rolfs.[9]

Now the average reader may be asking themselves, "Why does any of this concern me? I am not a board member of a church. I'm not a pastor of a church. Heck, I don't even regularly attend a 'traditional' church."

The answer, unfortunately, is even worse than what happened to the Crystal Cathedral. First, we need to realize that the Bible considers the true "Church" the body of believers, not an actual building or denomination. Second, when we look at the body of individual believers, the story, as I said, gets even worse. The leadership of Crystal Cathedral still had their own personal income and finances to sustain their lives and families. However, when it comes to financial failure in our personal lives there is much more at risk.

Here is where faithful individuals find themselves: Not only are their churches in debt, not only is leadership embracing faulty financial strategy that threatens the growth of existing believers and prevents the advancement of the Kingdom to those yet saved, but as individuals, believers are being bound as well!

The Shackle of Debt

Yes, bound. And while debt in and of itself is not *technically* a sin, Paul reminds us in Romans 13:8 to "owe no man any thing." The Bible is extremely careful to warn against, even going as far as bringing it up in the Prayer of all Prayers, The Lord's Prayer:

> *Our Father which art in heaven, Hallowed be thy name.*
> *Thy kingdom come, Thy will be done in earth, as it is in heaven.*
> *Give us this day our daily bread.*
> *And forgive us our debts, as we forgive our debtors.*
> *And lead us not into temptation, but deliver us from evil: For thine is the kingdom, and the power, and the glory, forever. Amen.*[10]

Notice how we are to pray for God to *forgive* us our debts! Notice, too, how we mention in our prayer "as we forgive others." After this prayer the Messiah continues to say: "For if ye forgive men their trespasses, your heavenly Father will also forgive you"[11]—referencing plainly the text about being forgiven as we forgive others.

Now there may be some that say the Messiah is clearly not talking about financial debt but rather sin, as sin places us in a spiritual debt to those we have sinned against. This is why some translations state "forgive us our sins as we forgive those who sin against us."

When we look at that in depth, we find that the Greek word used here is *opheilema*, a derivative of *opheilo*, which means to owe in debt morally *or* financially. This means that Biblically speaking, to owe someone financially is akin to sinning against them. Meaning that having debt is not something that would prevent you from Salvation, it is something though that goes beyond our thought of just money. Debt has moral and spiritual consequences to it, so much so that even sin that does require God's salvation is referred to in financial terms. So with this truth in mind, when a church of all entities enters into a debt relationship with a bank, it is willfully placing itself, its members, and its mission in a position of willful servitude and obligation to the lender. Now we could add in there a bunch of stuff about entering into an obligation with a lender who is not of the same faith, which the Bible calls "unequally yoked," and no, it does not refer just to marriage. However, I think the point is clear enough that debt is a major concern to the Father. And when a body of believers places the purpose and objective secondary to their desire to secure debt, not only is immature leadership a given, but sin is also a legitimate concern.

Debt Keeps Us from Being Our Mission

Let us go back to our story of the hero who *can* save the world, yet due to his or her own actions (and maybe ignorance) finds himself bound in a jail cell. As an ambassador for Elohim, the Church (as a collective and as individuals) is called to be a solution to a doomed world, to bring rescue from an unwanted future. They are charged with bringing the lost to Salvation and to bring leadership to the Saved on how to live in the world but not be of it. The Church cannot answer the call if it is shackled with debt. Regardless of how heartfelt the desire to save, believers cannot focus on the rescue of souls when they're held in bondage by debt, just like our hero could only sit in jail wishing and hoping he or she could do something.

The father of lies has been telling the elect that if they build a bigger church, bigger temple, or bigger synagogue, then more people will come. A large church usually has to compromise on what should not be compromised to "draw a crowd." This fact is amplified by the obvious call from the Word to go out to the world, not to bring the world into your building.

The astute will point out what I have already stated—that the Church is not a building or a denomination, but rather a body of believers. Some may inappropriately assume that the failings of many church buildings may be of no consequence to those believers who do not participate in corporate worship.

Strategically, that mindset is faulty. Yes, it is true that the Body is the actual church; brick and mortar are just things that will decay in the erosion of time. However, there is a need for a place where believers can come together, and that need is supported not only with historical evidence, from the first European settlers of North America to the persecuted Body of believers in places of modern-day persecution, but also with Biblical support as well—the disciples all knew coming together was vital to strength and strategy. Scripture reveals (Ezekiel 40–48, for example) that in the future there will be collective corporate worship in a designated temple building.

Also, while it is true that believers know that it is the individuals that make up the Body, nonbelievers do not. When they see church after church obtaining mortgages, filing bankruptcy, and renting space to nonbelieving companies to raise money, these nonbelievers who only see the building as the "church" are subtly turned off to your message of salvation—why would they believe you offer solutions to eternal problems when you don't even know how to deal with the financial problems and the ruin that comes from them, even though "money is not that important"? Instead, they see a body of people who seemingly cannot even handle the unimportant issue of money, while seeing no evidence of God's instructions in your professional efforts. So why would we even expect them to believe us when we talk about how to get rewarded in Heaven? This is true whether you attend a cathedral or a home-based church with family.

If nonbelievers do understand that the Church is composed of individuals, their perception of "the Church" actually gets worse, not better, because the majority of individual Christians are in bondage financially. Believers are called to be holy—set apart—but by and large we're not doing that financially, which prevents us from being an example of how His ways are different (and better) than the ways of the world. The majority of Americans have debt in the form of mortgages, student loans, car payments, credit cards, and the like, and with 80 percent being at or near the poverty level,[12] getting ahead of the debt is like swimming upstream…up a mountain. Missing just one paycheck would put most families into a financial tailspin, as two-thirds of American families live paycheck to paycheck.[13] What impression will nonbelievers have of the Church and the financial teachings offered therein when the average parishioner cannot write a check for $500 because, like most Americans, he or she doesn't even have that much saved?[14]

A constant battle with poverty. Very little, if anything, in savings. Paychecks eaten up by debt. No control over your time or decisions. No means to be generous, even to one's church. That is bondage!

Please understand that if you find yourself in this form of bondage, I don't mean to offend you. Lord knows that I have had times in my life where five bucks in my pocket was akin to feeling wealthy. My point is that as a body of believers we cannot ignore this any longer—*we need to swallow our pride and humbly admit that there is an epidemic placing believers in bondage.* Poor stewardship of money has placed nearly eight out of ten readers of this book in a financial jail cell—*and* a spiritual jail cell, because it hampers your witness and your work.

Forget the conversation about how to use money for good. Forget about talking about the love of money being the root of all evil. Forget about telling others that money is not the most important thing. When you are in debt, you have no real ability to participate in the discussion of money, be it for its good or evil uses.

Nor can you participate in the flow of money. You may hear of jailed believers in Libya who are being milked for bail money. If you are broke, you cannot help. You may be presented with the opportunity to send Bibles into North Korea. If you are in debt, you cannot help. A member of your church prays that God moves someone to give, so her husband can have a lifesaving procedure. If you are living paycheck to paycheck, you are not able to give.

Usually, at this point in the conversation, pride raises its ugly head and I hear an egotistical response like, "Josh, I give all I can." I understand that, and every penny helps, but when someone says that they give all they can, yet they do not study how they could make more to give, it tells the world that it is survival they are concerned with, and if there is something to give after that, so be it. I urge you to look past yourself as there are so many in need, in pain. Is the aforementioned fact that most of us only give of the crumbs left after our own survival true? Yes. Does it hurt your heart to realize you are in this position of bondage? Yes. And is it possible you are a pastor or leader in the Church, and you excuse away the pain of guilt you are now feeling by using Scripture out of context, since your "heart was in the right place?" Yes.

"Pride goeth before destruction, and a haughty spirit before a fall"—Proverbs 16:18

We need to swallow our pride and realize there are more than a billion believers around the world being held in this form of bondage, along with tens of thousands of houses of worship. Not to mention the financial and spiritual bondage of innumerable souls needing to hear the Word who will not be able to because we're allowing our resources to be limited. We all know that since Biblical times, it has taken money to send out missionaries or to distribute the Scriptures. We need to collectively put on our big boy pants and realize it is our lack of proper teaching regarding faith and its relationship to money that has led to a world in need—and has left the hero who could swoop in to save them stuck in a jail cell.

Learn from the Pain

Will the rest of the book cause pain and discomfort? Yes, some of it will. Because we have abdicated our role on faith and finance, the pain of truth will be present for most, but as I'm sure you know, the Truth shall set you free as well as heal the pain. The pain that may accompany learning the Truth is not punishment, but rather the ripping away of the blinders that years of lies have put upon you.

Maybe a half of a percent of the people reading this book can say that they give generously and that they have no bondage of debt. Yet they may falsely assume that they need not partake in the rest of the book. This would be an error that only amplifies the problem.

What about the people around you? What are you doing to help them? Do you realize the gravity of the situation? If you do happen to be in the top half of the wealthiest one percent (the percentage that experts agree don't personally need to worry about financial issues), and within your sphere of life and influence there are families being bound and torn by debt, your church has a mortgage, and you yourself have poor financial practices, then you are neither living nor teaching your faith. This, unfortunately for you, also means you are not doing what the Father desires; and not doing what the Father desires is...sin.

The bottom line is this: The "church," as individuals and/or a physical building of corporate worship, is in bondage. This bondage comes by our own ignorance and sinful nature. In a sense this is worse than if it were to come at the hands of the Romans, Alexander the Great, or the pharaohs of Egypt. Believers have believed not the Bible but rather the whispers of the evil one when he lied to us about what Elohim wants us to do with our faith and financial lives.

You have free will; the ties that bind are only but shadows of reality. The reality is that your financial solutions are not only Biblical but are within your reach. Not only are the binds that hold you back financially just a shadow, but so are the other ties that bind us in our hearts and spirit. The One who came to set you free did not limit that freedom to after death; He came to set you free in all Truth and we were given the Word to lead us in all our ways, ALL. When we trust the Word we can free ourselves and then set those around us free as well. The truth—knowing it and also acting on it—can set you free.

The good news is that there is hope for all of us. There are ways to break free from the bondage of debt, and yes, you have what it takes to do so. I understand many may be realizing for the first time the reality of their financial situation. Please know that whether you are five thousand or five million dollars in debt, you can do all things through the Messiah who strengthens you. Together we will get there, and the discomfort you may be feeling now will be but a motivating memory.

EVANGELPRENEUR ACTION STEP

Take a moment and do a self-check: What financial bondage do you find yourself in? Do you recognize it or have you grown so accustomed to it that you just see your bondage as part of life?

Take a look at your church, if you go to one, and ask yourself: Is financial bondage there? What does it look like? Is an unneeded expansion being built with borrowed money? Is the pastoral staff hoping a bigger building will be like the promise in *Field of Dreams*—if they build it, the people will come?

Once you start looking for financial bondage, you will see it everywhere!

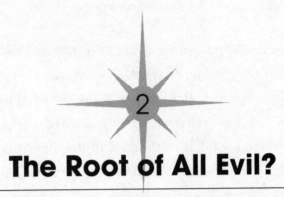

The Root of All Evil?

What Money Is and How It Is Loved

F WE'RE GOING to be Evangelpreneurs, then we need to not only be debt-free, but also we need to understand money's place in the world. How do you view money? Do you think it's the root of all evil?

"For the love of money is the root of all evil: which while some coveted after, they have erred from the faith, and pierced themselves through with many sorrows."
—*1 Timothy 6:10*

What a famous and misused bit of Scripture!

Usually when this Scripture sound bite is used, "the love of" is usually redacted, leaving us with the more often used phrase, "Money is the root of all evil."

Is money the root of all evil? Of course not. Is money the fruit of all goodness then? No, of course not. Money is neither good nor evil, it is just money. So before we dig too deeply, we need to define "money." What is it? Where does it come from? Are we supposed to avoid it since the love of it *is* the root of all evil?

Money is simply a tool, an economic device that allows us to trade and engage in economic activity. Today, money takes many forms, from gold and silver to fiat currency to internet "bits," such as Bitcoin and Worldcoin. Even time itself is being used as money now in a number of Western economies. For example, in Breckenridge, Colorado, Mountain Hours are used as a local form of currency valued by the worth given to one hour's worth of labor. Residents can use Mountain Hours as payment in town restaurants and other local businesses. And as of August 2020, there were even cities creating their own currency in order to recover economically from COVID-19.[15] It gives the people of the community more control over the value of items as well as a bit of protection against inflation.

I'll Trade Ya

The concept of money is simple: I have eggs that you want, you have furniture that Sally wants, and Sally has clothes that Jim wants. You and I could trade, but it would be messy. In order for you to get my eggs, you would have to talk me into taking your furniture, which I might not want at the time. Sally wants your furniture, but because you wanted my eggs more than you wanted

Sally's clothes, Sally is out of luck if you and I reach an agreement and I get your furniture. Also, since I don't really want your furniture, I might require more of it when you trade with me than Jim would require from you because he could trade it with Sally for the clothes she has and he wants—so the amount used to trade with each of us could vary widely. Not only that, but if you were to travel to another town you would have to take a lot of your furniture with you just to have enough to trade for all you need, such as food and lodging at your destination. Even then, you better hope they need your furniture and like it, or you will be out of luck. You can see the obvious problems here, and that is with only three products and four people. For millions of products and billions of people, this system just becomes impossible.

Then something called money comes along. Money, in its simplest form, makes the process much easier. The money is given a value (usually backed by a commonly accepted item with value, like gold), and then you decide how much your furniture, for example, is worth—let us say 76 money units for a table. I decide my cartons of eggs are each worth 2 money units. So if I want a table, but you don't want eggs, then instead of paying you with 38 cartons of eggs for your table, I can pay you 76 money units after I sell my eggs to someone who does want them. It is a bit more complicated than that when it comes to things like exchange rates, flexible valuations, and inflation, but as far as defining what money is, we are spot on.

Since that is what money is, then we can also say that it is a tool that allows us to accumulate items, and power over those with less of it, and that empowers mobility in a societal structure.

Is money evil? Of course not. It is as evil as a wrench or a toothbrush.

Loving Money

Now that we know that money is not evil, we have to look at what it means to love money.

How do you love your family?

- You spend time with him/her/them
- Take the pain for them so they are protected
- Your thoughts are captivated by them when they are not in your presence
- You are tender, kind, slow to anger, quick to forgive
- If you are a man, you sacrifice and live for your wife as Yeshua did for His bride
- Your dreams of the future revolve around them
- Late nights and early mornings are spent building and protecting your relationship with your family
- You purposely invest time and effort in your children so they grow to where you want them to be

- Your happiness is determined by the health of those relationships

We'll come back to our relationship with family, but first let's look at our relationship with money. I'm going to warn you—the following will be painful for most, but it is a pain that will shed truth on life, and again, it is worth it to be free.

Whenever we talk about money there is a word that comes up that seems synonymous with "money," and that word is "greed." We all have a mental picture of someone who loves money, someone who's greedy. The limo, top hat, big cigar, private jet, and extravagant jewels are usually among the images that flood the mind when the word "greed" is uttered. The man from the Monopoly board game or Daddy Warbucks from the musical *Annie* are personalities that personify "greed."

Is this the correct image, though?

Now that we know what love for family looks like, let's replace "family" with the word "money" and let's see what we get.

How do you love money?

- Spend time with it (making it, managing it)
- Taking the pain so it doesn't have to. Ever get up early to make money? Ever work through illness to make money?

- Do you ever get angry at money? No? Most of us get angry at and are slow to forgive those who don't give us as much money as we want or get in the way of us making more of it.
- Have you ever treated money as the Messiah treated His church? I know a lot of people who sweat, bleed, and cry over money only to have it reject them.
- Do your dreams of the future only come true if more money is in the picture?
- Do you ever get up early for money? Stay up late to make or worry about money issues?
- Do you invest time and energy growing your money? Compare the amount spent "raising" your money versus the amount of time raising your own children. How much time do you spend making money? How much time is left over for your spouse and kids?

I told you that it would be painful!

Actions speak louder than words, so let's take a look at common actions and you can discern for yourself where your love is.

Show Me the Money

When I go into a church or speak to a group of believers, they love to tell me that money is not the most important thing. I couldn't agree more, so I recently asked a men's group, what is the first question you have asked, or plan on asking, your daughter's fiancé when he asks for her hand in marriage? Do you know what the most common answer is across the Western world of believers? It is *not* "How long have you been walking with the Lord?" It is *not* "Do you have a plan on leading my daughter and grandchildren in their spiritual walk?" Do you know what the number-one question Christian/Jewish/Muslim fathers ask? Keep in mind that these are fathers who are believers, fathers who will tell you in a heartbeat that money is not the most important thing. They ask, "How do you plan on providing for my daughter?" Not even, "How do you know you love my daughter enough to be her husband?" Nope, the first question around the world is focused on money.

The number-one question is focusing on an issue that we tell ourselves is not the most important thing? Obviously, there is a problem.

Do you know what the second question often is? "How big of a wedding are you thinking of having?"

Sadly, when asking nonbelievers what their first question would be, I get, "When do you plan on having the wedding?" Again, not what I would think would be the most important, but a much better question than that of most believers! Not that the question of provision is not important—it is, which is why I wrote this book—but to a believer, questions like, "How long have you been a believer?" "Do you have a good prayer life?" "How long have you been going to church?" "What church do you go to?" all would be a better place to start when talking to the man who plans on marrying your daughter.

Believers, for a bunch of people who claim to not love money, sure are greed focused. Therein lies the problem: We don't really know what greed is.

Pretend for a minute that you are not reading this book and answer the following question honestly. Or, better yet, think of the people you know; how would they answer the following question?

"If you were to get a 10 percent raise at work, what would you do with the money?"

The most common answers I get are:

- I would get a bigger TV.
- I would take a vacation.
- I would get new rims for my truck.
- I would get an iPad.
- I would get new carpet.

We don't really know what greed is.

Nine out of ten times the answers revolve around what the person can buy for themselves. Part of what it means to love money is focusing on accumulating the stuff money allows you to gather.

This is where it gets interesting. When I ask people (and you can do the same) what would they do if I gave them a substantial amount of money, say $10 million or more? They say:

- I would quit working so hard (stop chasing money).
- I would get a private nurse for my aging parents.
- I would give to the children's hospital.
- I would build a homeless shelter.
- I would send a million Bibles into Third World nations.

Well, this is indeed interesting. When most people think about getting a substantial amount of money—what most would consider "too much" or "greedy" for them to keep for themselves—they think of ways to act with it that are not greedy at all. But when they think about getting just a little bit more than what they have—an amount nobody would consider "greedy"—they actually become greedy and selfish, thinking of ways to spend it on themselves. If this is you, don't feel too bad, you are in the same boat as most people around you. I used to be the same way. When you don't have enough for you, you are what you tend to think about. When you no longer have to worry about you, you have the ability to expand your vision. It just goes to show, though, how much work we have cut out for us; we have been living the wrong way (but calling it right) for generations now.

This means the vast majority of people, those with a heart and soul, are and have been using the non-Biblical definition of "love of money," which is really just the image of greed and/or accumulating wealth, as the common definition.

Yet, so wrong is the common definition that we don't even recognize greed when we live it out. Here is an example:

Sally goes to church, reads the Scriptures, and has a job at Road Runner Logistics. She goes into work early, leaving family behind in order to make money. She stays late for the extra $2 per hour in overtime. When offered time at work this weekend, she accepts, sadly missing her daughter's soccer game so she can make an extra 80 bucks after taxes. When a transfer opportunity is offered to her, one that would require her to move her family three hundred miles away, away from the kids' school, away from her friends, away from her and her husband's parents and siblings, she takes it because it pays more.

How much does it pay? Five dollars more per hour. An extra $200 a week, or $800 a month, was all it took for her to leave the most important things in order to "advance my family's financial situation." Eight hundred bucks! And that's before taxes.

Do not misunderstand me; I am all for doing whatever it takes to put food on the table and a roof over our heads. There are wonderful parents raising kids out of their cars as they work any job that will have them. Even though they may need to work long hours, they are doing what they can. I respect them for doing what they need to do, and it should be appreciated! A child raised in a tent city where his parents read the Scriptures to him and teach him the ways he should live has a much better life than a kid in an exclusive neighborhood with parents who ignore his upbringing.

My point is not that we should ignore our families' needs—we shouldn't—but that what we are doing many times is not the right thing, for us or our families, and in many cases it is actually the greedy thing to do because it only focuses on our needs and not the greater needs we, as believers, should be focusing on.

I remember once, after I gave a presentation, someone came up to me and said, "Josh, I don't need millions of dollars, I can get by very nicely on forty thousand a year." To which my response was, "That is great and I'm glad you have your needs met. There is a children's hospital in town, and that hospital needs more money to help more kids. There are unsaved people around the world who need to have a missionary share with them the Gospel, but the missionary needs money in order to go. If you care about God and others, life is not about what is enough for you, it is about living out God's purpose for your life, and a billion dollars, at that point, would not be 'enough' for you."

Working Hard for the Money

The problem is not that everyone needs to make a billion dollars in order for them to live out God's will for their life. Nor is the problem that if you make $70,000 with your needs met but no one else's that you must be greedy. Both assertions would be foolish.

Let me be clear: Your salvation has *nothing* to do with your income. You *cannot* buy a position in Heaven. You are *not* worth less if you don't have money. The point is that if you are working, you are working for money. If your employer stopped paying you, you would stop showing up. We also know that money, while not one of life's most important things, is still important, yet we pretend it is not, or pretend we don't need it, or couldn't use it. When we pretend these things we are living outside the will of God.

God uses rich people—look at the stories of Abraham, David, Solomon, Moses, and Joseph. He also uses poor people—for example, the poor widow with the two coins, Ruth, and the widow with only olive oil and flour who took care of Elijah. Nowhere does the Bible command us to take a vow of poverty. (If you are thinking of Yeshua's lesson regarding the rich man entering Heaven, see my discussion of this verse in its full context in the FAQ section of this book.) We are to work for a living. If we are to work for a living, it would be irresponsible for us not to want to do our best. If we do our best and we are not controlled by an employment situation, many times our best will lead to a certain amount of wealth. It's not bad, it's not evil, and it may come and go in seasons according to God's will for your particular life (Job and Joseph come to mind).

Greed, or too much money, really isn't the issue; the issue is engaging in revenue generation in such a manner that takes us away from the most important thing and replaces those things with a situation that abdicates time with family, time with God, or time pursuing your calling, and more often than not places you in a detrimental financial position.

This problem is not just that of the individual, either. Churches are falling for greed as well. Any church that has the audacity to ask for or accept money without teaching the proper perspective of money and its generation is ignorant at best, and if they continue to build on debt while they witness their congregation suffering financially, it is bordering on greed. Sadly, this is the vast majority of churches. No wonder so many are in financial trouble!

(T)he Bible talks more about money
than it does Heaven.

It is time we refocus our efforts and redefine "greed." The situation in which we find ourselves now is that we believe money isn't important, so we go about earning it in the wrong way (more on this later). However, because to us money really does have importance, we sacrifice time with God and family in order to get more of money, meanwhile failing to realize that while we are earning money, we are costing ourselves what we say is more valuable. Instead, we should realize that the Bible talks more about money than it does Heaven. The Bible tells us: "A good man leaveth an inheritance to his children's children" (Proverbs 13:22).

Newsflash: That is wealth! We have already covered how poverty is a curse and prosperity is a blessing. When four out of five churchgoing people are at or near poverty, are we experiencing the blessing or the curse? When most people don't have six hundred bucks in the bank, let alone the ability to leave an inheritance for two generations (his "children's children"), are we blessed or cursed? Wouldn't it be better, if instead of dancing around the issue or pretending it doesn't matter, or worse, blaming God for our lack of success, we approached money as a tool to accomplish our larger priorities and the goals associated with it?

EVANGELPRENEUR ACTION STEP

Since we are so ingrained in our perspective of money, we need to work on reexamining what money is, how we personally use it, and how we can use it in ways that would be outside of our normal routine. So, in the next twenty-four hours, do the following to expand your perspective a bit. It might seem a bit silly at first but it will give you a fresh perspective:

- Buy something for someone who is not expecting it.
- Donate money to a religious cause.
- Donate money to a political issue.
- Go on Craigslist or a similar site and barter. There are hundreds of people right now looking to engage in economic activity without using money, and it is great to experience how empowering that can be.
- Give money to a stranger directly.
- Sell something you own.

Yes, you can do all that in twenty-four hours! You do not need to use big amounts, either. You could accomplish the entire task list for less than the cost of this book. It is not about the amount but rather getting you to experience different uses for money in the shortest amount of time possible. Because we're in the rut of "Go to Work—Buy Groceries—Pay Bills—Tithe—Go To Work," we tend to forget what we can do with money. I promise, at the end of twenty-four hours you will feel great and you will have more awareness of the fact that money is a tool.

Getting Out of Debt Is Never Enough

Getting Rid of Debt Incorrectly Can Worsen the Problem

ABOUT TEN YEARS AGO there was a movement sweeping through the Church to eliminate debt. Houses of worship sold books, held studies, and formed ministries around the push to get debt out of the "Body." Millions of books on this topic sit on the shelves of millions of churchgoers around the world. Books were read and courses were attended.

Ten years later, where do we find ourselves? In more debt, in more foreclosures, in more bankruptcy, and in more depression.

The reason why should really not be a surprise to those with a calculator. (As a side note, I was predicting this unhappy result when the movement first began sweeping through the church. Not because I'm a prophet, but because getting out of debt is *never* enough!)

Isn't it sad that getting out of debt is now considered a major accomplishment in life? Indeed, when you're thousands or tens of thousands of dollars in debt, getting out of debt *is* a major accomplishment. But what makes it sad is that it is an accomplishment we shouldn't be pursuing in the first place—for we shouldn't be in debt! So crazy is this debt problem that there is even a radio show that has callers call in to celebrate the fact that they have finally made it out of debt. Again, congratulations, but it is sad nonetheless. Getting out of debt really means you are now at zero, back to owing nothing but also having nothing. So really we're considering being broke a financial victory. In racing terms, it's like celebrating that you finally made it to the starting line.

Let me again stress that if you are fighting to eliminate debt and you achieve your goal of getting back to zero, then I understand your reason for celebrating, but that celebration will be short lived. The reasons why we now find ourselves in more debt is because we are doing the same things that created the debt in the first place. No, I'm not referring to buying habits. People who believe changing their spending habits and "living below their means" is the path to sound financial stewardship don't really understand the situation. Will the practice eliminate debt? Possibly, if you happen to remain living long enough to achieve this goal. When we look at how many years this can take, how unhealthy employment can be, and our own age and personal health, there are many who engage in this action yet never live long enough to experience victory.

Why You Aren't Getting Ahead

Before we get to how we truly fix the problem, let us first realize how the problem gets worse. Many people have heard of the term "yo-yo diet" when it comes to losing weight. A yo-yo diet is when you reduce your caloric intake, burn more calories, and lose weight. Then, six months later you are ten pounds heavier than you were when you first started the diet.

Unfortunately, we experience similar results when we yo-yo debt. Millions of people who have eliminated debt in the past are now further in debt than they were when they first took the time and made the effort to eliminate their debt in the first place. They tried, and accomplished, getting out of debt—a great achievement, just like the man or woman who accomplished the weight loss. But just like with the weight coming back, so, too, does the debt.

To understand why the debt comes back we need to look at what course of action was taken to eliminate it in the first place. The first step most widely suggested and taken is cutting back on spending. A good start, no doubt. The second step usually taken is getting another job. Then comes eating franks and beans to cut spending even further, and then comes the spouse getting a second job as well.

The obvious problem with this is that it increases the number of evils and the level of risk in your life and the life of your family that are created by employment and time away from your priorities. More employment equals higher rates of heart attacks and cancer, divorce, pregnancy, and drug use among your children, and so on—all in the name of getting out of debt.[16] I am all for getting out of debt, but at what cost? Having debt can create problems, too, no doubt about that, but sometimes our efforts to eliminate debt actually amplify the problems we are trying to avoid in the first place. If debt is causing stress in your marriage and the family is sacrificing more time together in order to eliminate the debt, which in turn creates more stress in your marriage, did you accomplish the goal?

Let's say that you decide getting out of debt is so important that you are willing to take the risk and get those extra jobs, more hours, or what have you. Let us say also that you live long enough to see that debt eliminated. Your family sacrificed for the short term with the idea of having a better life long term. "Do today what others won't so you can do tomorrow what others can't," right? For a time, maybe.

The Bible clearly points out that debt is something we should avoid, and I obviously agree that getting out of debt should be an individual and family priority. A person in debt is a person without options who is servant to the lender. What I don't agree with is the method so commonly taught for how to get rid of this debt—employment.

For argument's sake, let us say you don't have to get two jobs, and your wife doesn't have to get two jobs, and you don't have to put in extra hours at work. Instead, you sold the boat you were making payments on, you told the kid down the street you would start mowing your own lawn, and you manage to get rid of the debt. Yay you! Now what?

This Isn't Your Grandfather's Dollar

Here enters the monster in the room: inflation. Inflation has had a practical yearly rate of about 10 percent for the past 100 years, give or take a point or two.[17] Inflation is one area where most people, including those who think they know what the economy is all about, tend to make a huge and costly mistake. The worst thing you could do is Google "yearly inflation rate" because it shows us nothing. That number is a calculation that reflects only choice indicators in the market. As a matter of fact, even the way inflation is officially calculated by the government has changed, and if you took a 2 percent reported inflation rate today and used the calculation they used before, the rate today would actually be 6–9 percent.[18] That is just as wrong, though, because even with the old math they were still only looking at certain market indicators, which they keenly selected and used in their calculations. Inflation is worthy of a book on its own and inflation isn't the only factor that erodes monetary value; other things that have to be calculated and considered are GDP minus lending, cost of living, devaluation of currency, trade deficit versus issuance of currency, artificially low interest rates to spur lending (Quantitative Easing, for example), PPI, CPI, MZM, wage and price controls, and domestic price growth. Even Congressman Ron Paul (R-TX) stated in an interview with Yahoo! Finance that CPI is not what should be used to determine inflation and that the government's inflation number is "rigged."[19] Congressman Paul, while grilling former Federal Reserve Chairman Ben Bernanke on this very issue of inflation, explained how even if we were just to use consumer price index (CPI), we would be at 9 percent annually (even though it was "officially" around 1.5 percent).[20]

In addition to all that, we have debt on the issuance of currency that does not get calculated into the equation. When the United States puts a dollar into the market, not only does it devalue the other dollars in the market, but we also instantly owe a debt on that dollar to the Federal Reserve Bank that printed it.

We can see the effects of inflation easily when we look backward. For example, in 1977, when I was born, the average household income of $11,992 when adjusted for inflation, according to the Census Bureau, is now worth $51,939.[21] However, if inflation were really only 2 percent a year it would mean that today, adjusted for 2 percent a year inflation, we would be seeing average household income of only $25,118. Keep in mind, household is combined income of all working adults at the address. In 1977 most household income was made of just *one* income earner. Today it is usually *two or more*, meaning this is much worse than most of us realize.

Most of us over the age of thirty have lived long enough to experience cost-of-living increases, but because that cost-of-living increase happens on so many things over so many years, we tend not to notice it. For example, who remembers that in 1995 a gallon of gas cost ninety cents? Almost impossible to believe, but it is true! Twenty years later we would still be below $2 a gallon if inflation was really only 4 percent a year—$1.97 per gallon to be precise. How many of us would think Heaven had come to earth if we woke up today and gas was $2 a gallon! In 1995 you would have been yelling at the television if the price went as high as $2; now $4 a gallon is becoming the norm and $3.50 per gallon is considered the common cost. Sure, oil is a commodity and more than just inflation is responsible for increased prices, but that only goes to further the point of this chapter: costs go up without your control and inflation is just one aspect of those rising costs. You have no control over the rising costs; shouldn't you have control over how your income can respond to those rising costs?

Consider this: A thirty-year mortgage that ends today started in 1985. Many people thought in 1985 that because they were making a decent wage and saving 10 percent a year, that it was the time to buy a home. But did they consider inflation? Did they think it was only 4 percent at the time and would mirror their rise in income? In 1985, the cost of the average home in America was $98,100.[22] In 1989 the same house was $148,800. Inflation is 3–4 percent a year, huh? In your dreams. In just four years, there was a cumulative gain of 11 percent per year in housing cost.

Now, you might be thinking that wages went up enough to compensate, right? Not even close. In 1985 the average household income was $23,620,[23] and in 1989 the average household income was $28,906. This means that while the cost of a home increased by more than 50 percent, income only went up about 22 percent—a 28-point gap. Another way to look at it: In just four years' time, a house went from costing 4.15 times the average household income to costing nearly 5.15 times. That is a practical financial backslide in only four years.

But could I just be pulling out a rare anomaly from decades ago? Did this terrible pattern continue?

Unfortunately it did! The average cost of a new home in America as of October 2014 (latest numbers available at the time of this printing) was $305,000.[24] Do not get excited and think, "Well, that is why it was smart to buy a house back then in 1985" because (1) the real estate bubble of 2008 shows otherwise, and (2) it is irrelevant, because this just further proves that income is *not* keeping up with increased costs.

Now, where are these people today? Those who took out a thirty-year mortgage in 1985 may now be underwater on that home, because in many cases their income did not keep up with costs and they used the equity in their home as a borrowing tool. What happens when you borrow and your source of income doesn't keep up with the rate at which the prices escalate? You go backward. In addition, when pensions and investments haven't kept up with inflation, long-term income in many cases hasn't kept up with long-term costs. Second mortgages to cover repairs, medical bills, or a number of other costs just add to this problem, not to mention rising property taxes. It has gotten so bad that according to a July 26, 2012, *NBC News* report, home prices fell 60 percent from 2006 to 2011 alone. In Arizona, 43 percent of home owners owed more on their mortgages than their homes were worth. In Florida that increased to 45 percent and in Nevada 61.2 percent of homes had loans on them for more than the home was worth.[25] We could get into a whole conversation about smart versus not-so-smart real estate investing, but the truth here is that we cannot count on employment and our cost-of-living increases to keep us from drowning financially.

People realized all of this in a more tangible way in 2020 and 2021 when, during the COVID-19 crisis, the idea of using home equity as a safety net proved useless. I remember one man with $400,000 in equity in his home who explained to me, in tears, that while he just needed $30,000 to get through a rough patch due to being laid off, the bank wouldn't give him a loan due to the fact he had no job and was living off credit cards. Thousands of other people similarly realized that the idea their home equity provided financial security is just ludicrous.

Through these examples we can see how household income has changed over the years and has not kept pace with rising expenses. Now, here is the real nail in the coffin: This is household income we are referring to! In 1985 a man could provide a home, a car, raise two kids, and have a stay-at-home wife all with the household income that he alone earned. Today the household income has two or three income earners and we still cannot make it. That means it is actually worse than I'm telling you!

These are just some common examples. We can look at food, clothing, rent, phone service, or what have you, and we also would find that your job is *not* going to be able to keep up with inflation. PERIOD!

Are You Counting on Your Retirement Plan?

Let me give you an example of an increase that is destroying family financial fluidity. Around the corner from me is a couple; he is a retired cop, she is a housewife. He is eighty-nine years old, she eighty-seven. They purchased their home in 1953, when he was twenty-nine years old and on the police force. The home cost $17,400 when he built it brand new. They thought it was okay, though, because he was bringing in nearly $70 a week after taxes. He listened to his financial planner talk about saving 10 percent and the "Rule of 72" (a method of calculating how much an investment has to gain each year to double over a given time period), and when he retired in 1970 with twenty-three years under his service belt, they had paid off their home. They were feeling good about it, too, because it was valued at $26,000 in 1970. Let us not forget that because of the mortgage, they paid more than that—$31,740 over the thirty years. Like most people back then, they believed that "real estate was always a good investment because it goes up."

By 2014, they had to move out of their home because they could no longer afford the property taxes of $250 per month—more than three times their house payment. Not to mention their retirement pension didn't keep up with inflation. Inflation, in the form of increased property tax, has forced this couple who were "middle class" in 1953 to move from their home because they could no longer afford to pay for a house that has been paid off since Nixon was in office.

So what does this mean? It means that if you do not get a 10 percent raise at work, you are actually going backward financially! After five years with no cost-of-living increase, you went backward 50 percent in real monetary value. If you get a 5 percent raise each year, you've still lost 25 percent of purchasing power in five years.

This is why most people, five years after eliminating debt, find themselves yo-yo debting beyond where they were before. The first time they eliminated debt they found areas in their life to cut costs and found things to sell. Now, all the cuts have been made, the extras have been sold, and the limited money from employment is just not enough. There also has been a rise in people using credit cards, which were once used on needless spending, to purchase food and basic household needs.

Keep in mind that as time marches on, the problem gets worse. A family will face more increases in costs and less potential from employment between 2021 and 2031 than a family did between 2010 and 2020. We went from one-income homes to two-income homes between 1970 and 1980. We cannot add a fourth or fifth income to homes in 2021. We are maxing out the income potential of employment and "side hustles."

This is why getting rid of debt is *never* enough. Instead, we have to get *ahead* of the inflationary wave. The only way to do that is through entrepreneurship! If we try to get more jobs to pay off debt, we then teach our children to get jobs to pay off debt, or worse yet, to go into debt for an education to gain employment in order to pay off debt. What this all means is we are just delaying and amplifying the inevitable through this accepted system of debt, debt elimination, and employment.

(For more information on how your dollar is losing value and an average return of 10–12 percent on your mutual fund is actually a rip off, read my other book, *Killing Poverty*.)

EVANGELPRENEUR ACTION STEP

Getting out of debt should be a priority—a lesser priority than other things, but a priority nonetheless. First, take out a blank piece of paper and write down all of your debts. It is surprising how many people do not really know how much debt they have, as they are afraid to really sit down and add it up.

Your debt needs to be eliminated. Selling things you don't need, cutting out expenses, and bringing in more money through entrepreneurship needs to happen. However, this next action step is for everyone, regardless of whether you have debt: Write down your income and, not accounting for the debt, write down your monthly expenses. Where are you? Now, be honest. Don't just list expenses you can afford with what you have left. List expenses you know you have or need to have. For example, clothing, gifts, travel, entertainment, new siding for the home next year, new driveway in ten years, lawn care—I mean EVERY-THING! There is no way this should be under $70,000 (see "The Practical Poverty Level" in chapter seven) for the year.

With what you make, now do this: Write down a year fifteen years in the future. Under that year write "Expenses," then take the list you have and increase the total by 50 percent. Then write "Income" and cut the total by 50 percent. And keep in mind that even these 50 percent adjustments don't depict things as bad as they truly are. If the income does not cover the expenses, I don't care how much debt you do not have—you need to change how you make money ASAP!

4

Who Really Controls You and Your Church?

If You Think It's You, You Are Wrong

W E'VE LOOKED AT DEBT, we've looked at money's role, and we've looked at how, even when you get to zero after getting out of debt, you're still treading water when it comes to finances. How do you get ahead? By becoming an Evangelpreneur, of course. But besides the practical financial side of being your own boss, there are also spiritual implications. It's about who you serve.

So let me ask you, who really controls you and your church? If you think it is you, you are in for a surprise.

Often people of faith point out that you cannot serve two masters. They also point out that we should give nobody control over our bodies, lives, or minds, for they belong to God; so much so that we are to renew our minds daily.

It is this idea of control that should send a shiver down your spine.

When Rome oversaw Judea, the Jewish king, Harod, was allowed to retain his authority within the Jewish land and law. We could easily make the case that Rome allowed this because it is easier to control people who believe they are free than it is to control people who are aware of their own captivity. Regardless of the reason, for a major portion of the Roman occupation, the Jewish people were largely "free"—free to engage in commerce, free to worship how they wished, free to have their own homes, free to pray to the One True God.

This of course changed to varying degrees after two events. The first event was the death of Harod, when his kingdom was divided among his three sons. The second event was the death, burial, resurrection, and ministry of Yeshua.

If we were to go back in time just before these two events and ask a rabbi who or what controlled the growth and effectiveness of his congregation, he would say, "God."

Likewise, we in the Western world assume that our churches, temples, synagogues, and lives are under the control of God. Ultimately, that is true, as He is divine and sovereign. However, we need to have a more mature look at this. If your child were in a class and didn't like math, she could say that because God is in control of her schooling and her life, if God wanted her to learn math He would give her that desire, make her homework easier, and so on. Does God control her class? Ultimately, yes. However, her teacher controls the class on a daily and directional basis, and we hope that God is in the teacher's heart. You would tell your daughter to listen to her teacher, do the work her teacher tells her to do, and listen to her teacher when it comes to manners in the classroom, would you not? Of course you would.

When Adam ate of the forbidden fruit, the keys to the Kingdom were given over to HaSatan (Satan), who had since been called the "god of this earth" and the "prince of the air." Even though God *is* sovereign, He allows consequences for our actions, be they natural consequences, such as driving drunk could lead to death, or spiritual consequences, like the Adversary influencing people, governments, and economies. If you hand over control of your mind to the media, for instance, you have to deal with those consequences, regardless of how long you have been a believer. You have allowed the media to be your god. I could go on and on—porn, sports, alcohol, and so forth—there are hundreds of idols and gods to which we hand control of our lives. So consider, who controls you, your family, and your church?

Are You Calling the Shots?

It would be easy (wrong, but easy) to assume that you have control over yourself. What if I were to tell you that your boss actually controls your life, and your family's life, and that your boss—along with the bosses of your church's congregational members—actually control the life of your church?

Don't believe me?

The decisions you make in life are in relation to the wages your boss pays you. Your wages limit your options.

What determines the house you live in? Your boss. What determines which school your kids attend? Your boss. What determines where you go on vacation? Your boss. What determines which clothes you purchase? Your boss. What determines the number of missionaries you can support? Your boss. What determines how much you can give? Your boss. What determines the quality of food you can purchase? Your boss. What determines the number of days you can take off to go on your mission trip? Your boss.

The examples goes on and on. Your entire life and ability to make an impact is determined by your employer. The same holds true in the lives of those with whom you attend church. I understand the tendency to be prideful and stubborn at this point, as realizing this fact is hard for many to take. Sadly, we again say this is God's doing—but, in 99 percent of the cases, it is not.

Since the issue is so sensitive, let me state again that money is not the most important thing. Our gross misunderstanding of how to use it places us in a position where others have more control over our lives than we do or than God does. Yes, we could make the argument that even entrepreneurs are affected by the economy. That's partly true, but devoid of the complete picture.

When you are an entrepreneur, you have the freedom and ability to shift with a changing economy, realizing that the "bad" times can actually be the most advantageous times. For example, if you owned a business in 1903 making horse-drawn carriages, you could decide to start working with a manufacturer of those newfangled internal combustion engines to start making horseless carriages, later to be known as automobiles. However, if you are an employee at a carriage maker and your boss decides not to change with the times, then your paycheck is going to end. It will have nothing to do with your work ethic or abilities; you simply had no control over your employer's decision to stay in carriage production. This same lack of control on your end holds true if your employer does decide to change with the times and starts making motorized carriages, but also decides to let you go and hire what they call a mechanic instead, who seems to be more suited to working on the new technology. Again, your income and everything affected by it was 100 percent in the control of your boss and 0 percent in your control.

Are you going to tell me God wants most of us to be voluntarily under the control of others? Sorry, but you need to sell blasphemous craziness somewhere else.

The Bible mentions four types of people: masters, laborers, servants, and slaves.

Masters and slaves are pretty easy to understand. A master is an entrepreneur, and with the blessing and guidance of Elohim, expands not only his business but also his ability to impact the areas of life that really matter to him and the One he serves.

Slaves, on the other hand, were considered property. In Biblical times slavery came about through war and people owing debt, and civil law commanded the owners to release their slaves after six years. They were never to be acquired from someone kidnapping and selling them—that was a crime punishable by death. It happened, though. Men, women, and children wrongly belonged to other men and were often treated as little more than livestock and had no option of freedom.

What about servants and laborers, though?

Laborers in the Bible are treated as independent contractors, a form of self-employment. If I am a laborer or independent contractor, and you are a farmer and you want your crops picked, you and I agree on a wage for the job. I complete the job, you pay me, and I move on. We negotiate the wage, hours, and terms. If you like the service I provide, you may want to hire me again, so it is in my benefit to do well. My future is in my hands, and if I want to learn new skills, I can make myself more desirable to those who may wish to secure my services. With a proper understanding of sound economic practices, I can even work my way up to master status. I have the ability to work hard, take time off, even relocate if I so desire.

Then there are the servants. They're not quite slaves, as they get wages and certain amount of liberty, yet they are not laborers either, as they have a set and limited form of earning, set hours, limited living conditions, and futures largely in the hands of their masters. Typically a servant in Biblical times would wear an article of clothing representing the master that he or she served. Today we call that a uniform or name tag. There was no end to the work. Unlike a laborer, who was paid and then free to move on to other pursuits when a task (e.g., rolling up fishing nets) was complete, when a servant was done with one task, he or she would be assigned another. As a servant, doing your work too well would lead to more toil without an increase in pay or freedom, and doing the work too poorly would lead to punishment. There were cases where servants could purchase their life back after years of servitude. Today we call that retirement. The servant could also decide to pledge the rest of his life to the master. This was usually symbolized by the master plunging a metal punch through the ear of the servant where an earring (similar to that of a slave) would be placed (see Deuteronomy 15:17). Today we call that "tenure" and "being fully vested." This form of servanthood is the same form referenced 136 times in the New Testament with the exception of only three verses that strongly differentiate themselves by the addition of the word "hired," as we see in Mark 1:20, Luke 15:17, Luke 15:19.

If we were to be honest, most of us would acknowledge we are servants. We are not slaves, not laborers, and certainly not masters. The sad thing is, unlike in Biblical times where servants became servants out of desperation, today we enter a similar arrangement not only voluntarily but by choice. To make matters worse, we teach our children to do the same thing.

A Servant's Life

As a laborer you have a customer to whom you provide a service, but you are free to control your time, mind, and money. However, being a servant is to be void of self and to have one's will replaced by the will of one who is in authority over you. This can be good when it is acts of kindness such as serving the Lord, or having a servant's heart, but the meaning is still present. God wants us to be laborers and masters, but does He want us to be servants?

Matthew 6:24 says: *"No man can serve two masters: for either he will hate the one, and love the other; or else he will hold to the one, and despise the other. Ye cannot serve God and mammon."*

Until the last sentence of that verse, we could make the argument that He is talking about Himself versus other gods (HaSatan, Jupiter, Easter/Ishtar, Ba'al, etc.), but then He says, "Ye cannot serve God and mammon" (money/wealth).

We have already discussed in this book how you *are* working for the money, how you *are* sacrificing time with God and family for money's sake, and now we just discovered you *are* most likely and voluntarily placing yourself in the position of a servant to your employer.

Scream, cry, puff your chest all you want. In your heart you know I'm right that many of us are guilty of this voluntary submission, which is why billions of faithful are facing the problems tied to money that we see. If I were wrong, we wouldn't be seeing the problems we are witnessing. As painful as that may be, it is true. Employment (servanthood) is not the way to dig your way out of debt. Being a laborer or master (entrepreneur, especially an Evangelpreneur) is.

Now, you may be thinking, "Josh, voluntary servitude has been around forever." The truth is, that is not actually the case, at least not to the scale in which we see it today. As a matter of fact, before the Industrial Revolution in the late 1800s, and more accurately, until inventions like mass electricity and the automated assembly lines, most people, with the exception of slaves and indentured servants, were entrepreneurs, laborers, or apprentices.

Apprentice? What is that? Today when we hear the word "apprentice," generally one of three images comes to mind: (a) the young boy helping out in Paul Revere's silversmith shop back in 1776, (b) a student Jedi from a Star Wars movie, or (c) President Donald Trump's former television show.

We will cover the role of an apprenticeship in our lives in the discussion of "saving the gravy" in chapter eighteen, but to define it, an apprentice was someone, usually younger than you, that you would take under your wing and instruct in your craft. An apprentice is not the same thing as an employee, for the purpose is for the apprentice to one day venture off on their own. An apprentice is also not a disciple, for a disciple is someone who puts himself in a position to learn how to live life entirely in a way taught to him or her by his mentor. Prayer, travel, food, God, interacting with others—all things pertaining to life are taught to a disciple. Just like an apprentice, slave, master, and servant, the modern Church has distorted the definition of "disciple" to mean a convert. Someone who "gets saved" and comes to Bible study is *not* a disciple. That, however, may need to be the subject matter of a whole other book.

Are You Unequally Yoked?

One final thing about who controls you and your life. We hear all the time about being unequally yoked when it comes to marriage. Sometimes we even hear about it when it comes to political actions and alliances. What about when it comes to employment?

"Be ye not unequally yoked together with unbelievers: for what fellowship hath righteousness with unrighteousness? and what communion hath light with darkness?"
—2 Corinthians 6:14

When you place yourself in a position of voluntary servitude—employment—you and your efforts are yoked to your employer. If your boss uses his money to buy hookers in Mexico, you empowered that. If your boss runs drugs out of the office, you empowered that (and may even be legally responsible). If your boss gives profits you helped create to abortion clinics, you empowered that.

No, you do not make those decisions, and ultimately the consequences fall on your boss, but your hard work *is* empowering the employer to which you have voluntarily yoked yourself. The case could be made that this is true of laborers too, because their efforts affect the one paying them and vice versa; however, as a laborer there is more freedom to choose and control the circumstances as well as terminate them with the freedom to pursue more beneficial agreements elsewhere. Whereas a servant, because of debt, bills, or limited ability has far less opportunity to unyoke themselves from their master/ employer.

In the Biblical example of servants, they were forcibly yoked to their employer. What does it say about us when we voluntarily yoke ourselves to an employer without even researching who we are serving for forty (and often forty-plus) hours a week?

It would be a safe bet to say that most employees who are also believers do not know who they are yoked to, nor did that factor ever come into consideration when applying for the job. They are just like a father who says money isn't important, yet the first question he asks his daughter's fiancé has to do with money.

Is it not time we took back control of our lives and became yoked to those who serve God?

EVANGELPRENEUR ACTION STEP

I want you to dream a little bit. If you have been in the workforce for more than five years, the idea of dreaming starts to die, and it is time we got it back. These are not going to be outlandish dreams. I'm not talking about Ferraris and mansions. Just start simple.

If you doubled your income and cut your time commitment for work in half, what would change in your life? Don't just smile and look off in the distance; write it down. Take the list of real expenses you wrote in chapter three and see what would change. Ask yourself, where would you live instead? How much control of your life would you have? Yes, giving is good and I want you to, but the point of this action step is to really get you to recognize the control everyone else has over your life and what it would feel like to take that control back.

Unanswered Prayers

Is God the Reason or the Excuse for Financial Hardship?

THERE IS A LINE in the Garth Brooks' song "Unanswered Prayers" that goes, "Sometimes I thank God for unanswered prayers...just because he may not answer doesn't mean he don't care."

With the exception of the grammatical error of using "don't" instead of "doesn't," the line is a good one. He is referring to how he asked God for this girl back in high school, and if God had granted the pairing he had prayed for, the young man never would have married the woman he is now thankful to have as his wife.

Should we, like the character in Garth's song, be thankful for unanswered prayers?

We should be thankful for God's providence and wisdom. If that means He does not answer every prayer we submit to His throne, we should be thankful. I believe we should be thankful for the privilege to pray in the first place. The fact that the Creator of all would be willing, and wanting, to hear from us is a miracle in and of itself that continues to leave me in humble awe. Too often "believers" view God as a cosmic genie, there to answer a wish. Prayers are not wishes. In His wisdom He cares for us and, at times, that care comes in the form of not getting what we want.

Good parents do the same. When your eight-year-old wants a tattoo of a Disney character, you wouldn't just say yes because they asked, would you? Of course not. Your wisdom provides you with the ability to make the judgment based on the child's best future interests. Your wisdom also allows you to project (to a much lesser extent than God) what the future desires of the child would be. You can be sure with 99 percent accuracy that when the child is eighteen years old, he would not want what he wanted at eight. Elohim happens to be much wiser than any earthly parent.

However, I know for a fact that we too often use God, and his judgment, as excuses for our failures and wrong actions!

(W)e too often use God, and his judgment,
as excuses for our failures
and wrong actions!

Did God Tell You to Be at Your Job?

I cannot tell you how many times people have told me, "Josh, I am working at XYZ Corp. because God wants me there." Now, I am the first to admit that God does indeed work in mysterious ways and He certainly has asked people to do some amazing and odd things. However, with that said, we need a bit of a reality check.

Let me give you an example to illustrate my point that people inappropriately credit or blame God for things He doesn't do. If you attend some churches, you will undoubtedly find a number of them have a large percentage of their congregation that seems to talk to God more than Moses did! And they quote God for mundane things, like, "The Lord told me he wants me to plant pumpkins this year." Or, "The Lord told me he doesn't like the sauce you use on your BBQ, and if you used Bob's you would sell more." It seems that some people hear from God so much it is as if God is a really bored girlfriend who has nothing to do and decides to talk to you more than two teenage girls do between classes.

I am *not* saying God cannot talk to people if He so desires, but these people hear from God so often that it makes the Bible look like the footnote of His conversation with humanity.

I am hopeful that most people reading this do not claim to hear from God as often as those people I referenced, and if you do, I hope you reexamine who it is you may really be hearing from. My point here is, we tend to give credit, blame, or excuses in the name of God rather than looking at the true source, and while you may agree that people claiming to hear from God about "Sally wearing the wrong shoes" is absurd, millions of believers are doing the same equally irresponsible thing when it comes to their financial lives.

There are so many people who tell me God wants them in this particular job or God has placed them with a particular employer, and while I am *not* saying that never happens, it is usually not the case, just like it's not usually God when people say they're always hearing from God.

Let's Look at Pete

Let us build an example together. Let us say Pete works for Acme Anvils. He works forty hours a week, commutes thirty minutes each direction, and gets an hour for lunch. This means he is away from his family for fifty hours a week. We ask Pete about his job, and he tells us, "I believe God placed me in this position." We start digging a little deeper and find he also travels away from home for work about four weeks a year. Not bad, but still, four weeks is an entire month out of the year that Pete is away from home. Pete is average, just like those profiled in a May 2010 article in the *Independent*, a newspaper and website out of the UK, which cited that the average family spends forty-nine minutes together each day; thirty-four minutes is spent with the kids, leaving fifteen minutes of wife-and-husband alone time![26] *Fifteen minutes!*

Despite all the time he spends away from his family for work, Pete tells us that Acme Anvils is where God has placed him. He believes that a job that allows him to spend the average of forty-nine minutes a day with his family and only fifteen minutes alone with his wife each day is God's will for him. Yes, people really try to convince themselves that God, the God who said in 1 Timothy that a believer should have their family and personal life in order before taking on ministry positions, wants them to spend only fifteen minutes a day with their spouse. Throughout the Bible, God places one's family life as a priority above ministry work.

Yet, here we are with Pete trying to say that God has placed him in a position where he gets to spend thirty-four minutes with the kids, fifteen minutes with his wife, and usually close to zero minutes with God. Does this mean that God has placed Pete's job above God?

Usually, at this point, the defensive claws come out, and the response is either (a) Pete has to provide for his family and God wants that, for it says 2 Thessalonians 3:10 *"that if any would not work, neither should he eat"* or (b) God is using Pete to spread the Gospel at Acme Anvils.

Spreading the Gospel at Work?

Let us deal with the latter first. Does God use Pete to spread the Gospel at work? Maybe. Let us first admit that most churchgoing "believers" do *not* actually share their faith with anyone, especially with those at work. According to the Barna Group poll from December 2013, only 52 percent of "believers" shared their faith with *one* person in the past year![27] The same study found that the less someone makes the more likely they are to spread the Gospel to one person, and the more someone makes the less likely they are to spread the Gospel to even one person. Should we hope Pete does poorly at work just to increase the odds of Pete spreading God's word?

(O)nly 52 percent of "believers" shared their faith with *one* person in the past year!

Also, let us be honest for a minute. If Barna Group polled you about spreading your faith, and you know, as a believer, you are called to do that very thing, would you fib and say you did even if you didn't? It would surely be a temptation. So I would guess that the number of believers who do *not* share their faith is much, much higher than 48 percent.

Thus, when Pete and those like him say, "God wants me to be there because I am a witness unto Him" when most believers aren't sharing the Gospel—and even those who are only share it with one person—they are wrong.

Are you ready for the real kicker? The study did not ask if the "believer" actually told someone at *work* of their faith or if it was a stranger at the bowling alley. Logically, we could assume that if we added that factor to the scenario, the case for Pete's rationale for his work goes down even further.

Pete works a job that requires travel. That usually means he makes more than $39,000. So now his odds of telling someone about his faith drop to 37 percent, as the Barna Group study also found that if you make more than $39,000 a year you are less likely to share your faith.[28] Pete has a few kids, which means he is probably over twenty-five years old. The study found that once someone is over twenty-five the odds of telling another person of their faith drops further still. Add to this the fact that even if he does defy the odds and shares his faith with one person, it is most likely not a coworker, and all of a sudden this excuse of "God wants me at this job to spread the Gospel" goes from a great calling to evidence that Pete is not even close to doing what he thinks God wants him to do.

This is where we get to Pete and his unanswered prayers. Pete, like you, me, and most people, has the best intentions in the world. We don't want our families to suffer, we don't want to have bad marriages, we don't want all the negative that comes along with the life we most likely are living in terms of our economic reality. However, when we truly ask the Father what He wants us to be doing, are we living as though He answered the prayer, or are we living as though we answered it for Him? As hard as it may be to admit, and I'm not singling out just you, we need to really pray and ask Him if we are doing what He wants us to do and for how long, too. If you are eighteen years old and paying your way through school, yes, He may want you working at the church as a janitor for a low wage. You learn a work ethic and how to budget, and you are given the freedom to concentrate on your studies as opposed to worrying about starting and growing a business. However, are you still praying two years later, asking for guidance when school is over?

Are We Settling and Calling It Answered Prayer?

What most of us will find is we are not as lucky as the guy Garth Brooks is referencing in his song. In our hearts we know we should be with the wife we were meant to be with, "wife" in this case being an economic life where we control the time, money, input, and output of our finances as well as being able to respond to God's other callings, not bound by traditional employment. Instead we didn't pray and we took the "girlfriend" we had before, afraid to walk out on faith and truly answer the tugging in our heart He has placed within us. Consider that more than 62 percent of Americans age eighteen to sixty-four would like to be entrepreneurs, according to an April 2005 Gallup poll,[29] and in an even more recent Harris Interactive poll in 2012, 91 percent of adults know that small business ownership is important to economic recovery.[30] So, in short, we settled. We then tell ourselves that what we settled for was God's answer, when in reality we are living out unanswered and often unasked prayers.

We need to consider two additional factors that affect people's ability to share their faith at the workplace: Most employers in the United States now ban all discussion of religious matters between fellow workers at the workplace and disallow the distribution of religious materials. So, even if Pete has that 50 percent chance of being bold with even one person, he is violating his workplace rules if he does so while on the clock. While I would tell people their first loyalty belongs to their Messiah and He has called us to spread the Gospel, the reality is that if Pete really does this to the extent to justify the lack of time spent with God and family, he would actually lose the job "God placed him in."

EVANGELPRENEUR ACTION STEP

Have you been using God as an excuse for anything in your life? Are you telling people that God placed you in your job, yet you haven't been using that job to do the one thing God wants you to do most?

Just taking the time to examine your life in this way is a huge step forward.

Does YHVH (God) Love Murder?

Taking the God Excuse Too Far

ET US PUT PETE ASIDE for a second and talk about Bob. Bob is doing time in an upstate prison for murder. Turns out Bob didn't take too kindly to his wife cheating on him, so he took out a knife from the kitchen drawer and slit his wife's throat from ear to ear. He is now facing ten years in prison (he would be facing thirty-five if he would have been doing drugs instead of killing people, but that's just the way it goes). While in prison, Bob hears the Gospel. So moved is Bob that he hits his knees, repents of his sins, and turns his mortal and eternal life over to Jesus. Now that Bob has done this and Jesus is his Lord and Savior, is Bob going to Heaven? If his conversion is true...yes!

Now, let's say two years go by and Bob is leading a prison ministry from behind bars. In the past twenty-four months he has lead thirty men to know the Truth of God's word and accept Yeshua as their Messiah. If Bob were to come to you and say, "God has placed me in this prison in order that I can lead so many to Salvation, and killing my wife was what God wanted me to do so I could be cleansed of that sin and lead so many others to His Truth," what would you say? Obviously you would object. God did not want Bob to sin by committing murder in order to go to prison and, while there, save people! God instead used that bad situation to work His will *regardless* of the situation!

Too often believers pervert Romans 8:28: *"And we know that all things work together for good to them that love God, to them who are the called according to his purpose."*

We take that verse and turn it into something like, "All things work to the Glory of God so anything I do is okay."

Notice that Romans 8:28 says "for good to them that LOVE God." Let us look at the Bible's definition of love:

"If ye love me, keep my commandments." —*John 14:15*

We all know that God commands His people not to murder, so it would be ludicrous to believe that God would want someone to commit the sin of murder just to have a situation that God could use to His Glory or to benefit the sinner. God may use a bad situation *regardless* of the circumstances that created that situation, and that is entirely up to Him and His will, grace, mercy, and providence. We must be thankful for His grace and mercy in those bad or sinful situations, not use those situations to teach how to behave as believers.

Yes, that is an extreme example, but it is true and easy to understand. What is not so easy to understand is that the same process and logic applies to Pete's situation from the previous chapter! Does God want Pete to spend just fifteen minutes a day with the woman God calls Pete's "one flesh"? No! Does God want the increased risk to Pete's family that comes with only spending thirty-four minutes with his children in order for Pete to work at Acme Anvils? No! Does God want Pete to be in debt? No! Does God want Pete to be led into temptation at work to have an affair (most affairs happen at work)? No! Does God want Pete to be in poverty? No! As a matter of fact Deuteronomy even calls poverty a curse (see Deuteronomy 28:16–68)!

Do you really believe that Elohim wants Pete to do bad things in order to save someone, or is it more likely that, just like in Bob's situation, God would use Pete *regardless* of the situation in order to save someone?

When you put pride aside, pick up the Bible, and use your logic and reason, the answer is blaringly obvious. God would never want Pete to sin and to be cursed in order to tell *maybe* one person in a year that God is real (see preceding discussion of Pete's reasons for staying at Acme Anvils).

We could make the argument that God is so great and He cares so much that He would see Pete through those sinful situations in order to save even one lost soul. However, that argument would be void of sound logic and reason. If God were to do that for one soul, could he not have Pete open up his own business and hire everyone in Acme Anvils? God could have a tract float through the breeze on a windy day to rest upon the feet of that one person Pete could lead to Salvation. After all, it is God who truly saves anyway! We tend not to remember that it is God who wishes that no one would perish and that it is His Spirit that is ultimately revealing the Truth:

"And Simon Peter answered and said, Thou art the Christ, the Son of the living God.

"And Jesus answered and said unto him, Blessed art thou, Simon Barjona: for flesh and blood hath not revealed it unto thee, but my Father which is in heaven."
—*Matthew 16:16–17*

Is It Really God's Fault?

Too often we do not want to live up to our responsibility in a situation, so we blame God and then, with a divine twist of logic, we can use God's providence as an easy scapegoat.

Many people point to Job (pronounced Joeb) and say, "See, God doesn't always answer prayers, Job suffered," and we also could point to Moses suffering in the desert after being exiled from Egypt. We could point to Yeshua Himself being tempted in the wilderness as an example of God not wanting things to go great. We could easily say, "See, he wants me to have the job, he wants me to have the debt, the bad marriage, the poor family life, the lack of time spent in His word, the inability to live out the calling He has placed in my life because we see the same examples from people in the Bible." Again though, this argument would be void of logic and reason.

Job, Moses, Yeshua, Paul, Peter, Noah, and every other example you find in the Scripture all face hard times and are not always perfect, but they do *not* do what God hates in order to accomplish their God-given objectives! Instead what we see are people going through trials and tribulations *while* living out a Godly life and objectives.

Just let me be clear: I am *not* saying that if you have a job that you are sinning. I believe that there are times and seasons in life and, for most of us, employment plays a role in a variety of parts and lengths of our lives. I am also not saying that you have to be an entrepreneur in order to be saved or be used by God. What I am saying is if we truthfully examine not only how God uses economics but also what we really feel our calling is, we would realize that for the vast majority of His people, employment is *not* where God really wants you. Instead we find ourselves making excuses.

Does God Want You at Your Job?

Consider the following:

Most jobs have:	Does God want this?
Excessive time away	No
Limits on spreading His Word	No
High affair rate	No
High divorce rate	No
High death rate	No
High poverty rate	No
High debt rate	No
Poor health	No
Limited ability to give	No

For most of us, God does not want us to be employed for the duration of our working lives!

Is it possible that in your specific case God wants you to be an employee? Sure. As I stated, there are times and seasons for employment. I believe that if God wants you to be an employee then He will provide confirmations of His will. Remember though, saved souls are *not* confirmation, but rather a result of His will being lived out regardless.

As we will discover throughout the course of this book, many people are ignoring the calling and power behind "Evangelpreneurship." Until the Church collectively and individually shifts its views of faith and finance in a way that lines up with God's provided example in His Word, we should expect nothing less than death and destruction, which the Church is experiencing today.

The wrong thing done with the right attitude does not make the wrong thing the right thing. Unfortunately that is the approach many of the faithful are not only taking but are also teaching. Let us change that.

EVANGELPRENEUR ACTION STEP

Do a little bit of self-examination. Where did you get the teaching that you should get a job? Honestly, where did that come from? Did nobody tell you to, and you just witnessed everyone around you doing it, so you did too? Did your father talk about how important it is that you get a job young and learn to be a man? Was it the media always talking about the job market? There is no right or wrong answer here; just really ask yourself where this message came from.

Along the same lines, ask yourself if anyone ever told you to be a business owner. What you do know about business ownership—where did that come from? What has your pastor taught about employment? Has he really taught anything other than to be a good employee? What has your pastor taught on being a business owner? He may support the idea and point out business owners in the church, but I mean what has he taught regarding why you should or shouldn't do it, and how to go about it?

Again, no right or wrong answers and no pointing blame. I want you to realize how these messages are not really taught one way or the other; they just kind of . . . exist. If we think about that though, how terrible it is. Here we spend most of our waking day doing something that nobody really is teaching, yet nobody can really figure out where the ideas came from.

PART 2

You've Got This: Don't Believe the Lies

7

Lie of the Devil #1: Get Rich Slowly

How This Is Mathematically Impossible

B Y NOW WE REALIZE that employment and our common practices of financial management do not place us in the position that God truly desires. We know that we have been using Elohim as an excuse when in reality we have been operating contrarily to what He teaches. We know we are handing over control of our lives and the lives of our families to lenders and employers who limit our ability in all areas of life. This realization will inspire many of us to become entrepreneurs. Or, more appropriately, *Evangelpreneurs*, as we live out the life God calls us to live while empowering that life with free enterprise.

Once people realize that they need to become Evangelpreneurs, HaSatan will follow. The Devil tells us that we are not cut out for it, that we don't have what it takes, and a number of other lies. In this section of the book we will destroy most of his lies, starting with the lie that we will get rich slowly.

When the Devil appears in the Bible, he always uses half-truths to convince people that his way is the right way. We have discovered already that when people don't have control of their time and money, they have handed over control to everyone and everything other than themselves and the Elohim they serve.

A Recap on Money's Role

As I've noted, money is not the most important thing in life. We try to convince ourselves that money is not important, yet we spend the majority of our waking hours making money. That doesn't mean that money *is* the most important thing, it just means we lie to ourselves because we spend most of our time making money, worrying about money, and suffering from the lack of and mismanagement of money.

Since we can maturely acknowledge that money does indeed play a role in our lives, if we do our best in our craft, then money will most likely increase.

So, let's talk about what we do with money.

If you were raising a fifteen-year-old who had a part-time job in order to buy a car next year, would you tell that child to quit and volunteer at a soup kitchen instead? He would still learn a work ethic and he could work for no money, so he wouldn't have to deal with that evil green paper. Yeah, it sounds stupid, doesn't it? If he wants a car by the time he is sixteen, he needs to do paid work and save the money. You've taught him that the Bible says that if a man does not work he does not eat.

You and your child are both on the same page: work for money, save for a car. God, family, and grades come before work, but work has become an important factor to your young man.

Now it comes to the savings.

If he is working for money and his goal is to save for a car, what would you say to him if he went to a ball-game with his buddies this past weekend and spent a bunch of money, and is planning next weekend to go on a ski trip that will cost even more? He is obviously not being what Christians would call a "good steward," for a steward oversees resources and assets in a manner that makes those resources and assets serve a higher agenda.

It is easy to see the problems in a teen and be critical of his actions, but let's take a look at our adult lives.

When we work, we do it for two basic reasons: to have money now (hopefully for Godly purposes) and to save money—or more accurately, to use money for long-term planning purposes (which also serve God).

Thus we need to take a long-term look at what we are doing with our money, as well as with our time and our lives as a whole.

Is Our Approach to Work Any Different than a Nonbeliever's?

The Bible says that we are to provide for ourselves, our children, and our children's children (Proverbs 13:22). In order to financially provide for three generations, we need to take a look at what the world teaches in terms of how we should go about doing that. Then we need to examine whether what we are doing is working, and if it is not working, we need to look at what we as believers are doing to make sure it is not the same as what the world teaches. What does each purport?

The World: Working forty hours (or more) a week trading time for money. Terms and practices such as Roth IRAs, 401(k)s, CDs, index funds, and the Rule of 72 are used in the pursuit of wealth for retirement as well as securing the wealth for two more generations to come. The result of following this way: Four out of five people are at or near poverty level, and savings are less than 1 percent of income.

The Church: Work forty hours (or more) a week trading time for money. Terms and practices such as Roth IRAs, 401(k)s, CDs, index funds, and the Rule of 72 are used in the pursuit of wealth for retirement as well as securing the wealth for two more generations to come. The result of following this way: Four out of five people are at or near poverty level, and savings are less than 1 percent of income.

Let's see if it is working.

In a MainStreet article, Carrie Schwab-Pomerantz from the Charles Schwab Foundation lets us know that if you are more than fifty years old now and do not have significant savings, retirement for you in the traditional sense is "unrealistic."[31] That same article suggests that you will need $2.5 million in order to retire.[32] A CNNMoney article from 2012 even suggests you may need $4 million to retire in the near future.[33] A 2014 Yahoo! Finance article pointed out that according to David Marotta of Marotta Wealth Management, someone who was then twenty-year-old would need to save up $7 million for retirement.[34] Mr. Marotta pointed out that this amount in retirement for someone who was twenty years old that year (turning 65 in the year 2060) is the financial equivalent of $166,000 in purchasing power in 1979. Keep in mind, too, that by the publication of this book's second edition in 2021, the seven million needed had already risen to ten million.[35] Obviously it goes without saying that unless you make a yearly income of over $300,000 your odds of saving up $10 million are pretty much zero.

It is important to note also that, as of 2021, the majority of people making $100,000 a year are struggling financially and 32 percent of people making $200,000 or more are running out of money before they run out of month. It is time we realize that while $100,000 a year might have sounded like a lot when you were growing up, time has degraded $100k to what $40k used to be.[36]

Whenever I talk about this topic on the air or to live audiences, I always get that person who reminds me that being rich is not the most important thing, and they are so right. This is not about being rich; this is about what works and what doesn't.

It Was Good While It Lasted

Economically speaking, no trend lasts longer than three generations. Let's look back to 1933 and the formation of what we now refer to as the "middle class," which developed after the New Deal, especially during World War II and the post-war era. The first generation of this trend had a great time. They earned a decent living, took month-long vacations, and retired in relative comfort in Florida, and when this generation passed away there was money for the kids.

That next generation that came along, those who are now in their fifties and sixties, were taught to do the same thing. In their early working lives this process worked, too, albeit less successfully. A father could support his family, own a home, pay off the car, and save for a bit of college tuition for his kids. However, unlike the previous generation, *gone* is the savings, *gone* is the retirement (which is why so many "retired" people are working), *gone* is the second home in Florida. Instead, there are long-term care costs that will bankrupt them, leaving their homes underwater and reversing mortgages. As a Huffington Post story pointed out, all the wealth accumulated by the middle class after 1940 is gone—all of it![37] Those counting on employment to elevate a people group (the middle class) out of poverty permanently don't understand how economics work.

Now let's look at the third generation, the ones who are twenty- to thirty-year-olds at the time of this publishing. Both husband and wife *have to* work, and secondary part-time jobs are common. The college debt of this generation is more than $1 *trillion*, and financial experts say that the student loan debt is going to be the next bubble to burst. This generation faces a future that places them in a worse position financially as a whole than the previous generation, which is now aging and larger in number. As a result, taxes are increasing to cover the programs created for the older generation, such as Social Security and Medicare. By the time an individual's college debt is paid, there is little time to prepare for retirement, let alone the care of their aging parents, which in today's dollars is $50,000 to $75,000 a year. What is that cost going to be twenty to thirty years from now when people of the third generation themselves need that care?

Because of these financial stresses, this third generation is not even hitting reproductive replacement numbers in terms of birth rate. This low reproductive rate is now a trend two generations deep and will have catastrophic effects on the economy in twenty-five years. This generation is even being told not to plan on being able to retire at all. (We will take a look at proper retirement and how the world has the wrong idea on this time of life in chapter eighteen.)

For goodness' sake, an executive of one of the largest financial-planning firms in the United States on a conference call with me and some other business leaders said if this generation wants to retire with a lifestyle equivalent to $60,000 gross a year in today's money, they have to put $5,000 into savings per month now. The only problem is that even if you make $60,000 a year now, you cannot afford to put away $5,000 per month net because it is not mathematically possible.

So what causes this? An employment-based economy governed and controlled by inflation.

The Practical Poverty Level

The following is a revised version of an article I published in 2011 called "The Practical Poverty Level."[38]

It has served as an eye-opener to tens of thousands of people and it serves as a good jumping-off point to get to the root of the problem and the heart of the solution. Remember, this was back in 2011.

Officially, the poverty level in America (according to the Department of Health and Human Services) for a single person is $10,830 a year, but for a while now I have found that number a little suspicious, since I know people who make much more than that and yet they are struggling all the time. What I have outlined below is what I am calling "Practical Poverty Level." What is practical poverty? It is the amount of money the average American would need to make in order to have NO money left for basic living expenses after paying the foundational expenses.

I have listed the twelve foundational expenses that most people have in their lives as single individuals with a college education. Obviously, there are areas in this list that may be lower for you personally and others that are drastically higher; all that means is that your personal poverty level would need to be adjusted to fit your life. However, do not let the fact that your bills are higher/lower distract you from the power of what you are about to read, because this IS what most people are facing and exactly why the world is in the financial situation it currently finds itself. This article should alarm and shock every reader!

The Monthly Foundational Basics

Housing	$1,000
Car Insurance	$144.66
Cell Phone	$73
Utilities	$264.33
Cable/Internet	$100.63
Food	$332
Gas	$220
Car Payment	$466
Savings for retirement	$395
College loan payment	$575
Life Insurance	$33
Health Insurance	$402

As you can see, there is nothing "excessive" on this list and I know we can all agree that this looks pretty basic and sound. Do you know what this means? It means you need to make, as a single adult, $69,600 a year ($70 grand) **before taxes** in order to have NO money left over! Let me say it again:

THE PRACTICAL POVERTY LEVEL FOR MOST AMERICANS IS $70,000.

The before-taxes part really is key to understanding this. If you take the expenses and do the math you will find that it is $47,961 a year, and you might be thinking, that is not $70,000. However, you can only spend what you have, which is called "net," and in order to net $47,961 you need to make a bit over $70,000 actually. Federal income taxes on that are 25 percent, state income taxes (which vary by state) will be anywhere from 4 percent to 5 percent, and all those items listed with the exception of food in some states will have sales taxes ranging from 5 to 10 beyond their listed costs. Yes, rent could offer a partial tax deduction, as could an education payment, but deductions only increase the return you get, not the monthly amount you have to pay first, meaning you have to pay it before you get it back. Besides, you should NEVER budget based on what you expect to get back in the form of a tax return.

If we were to look at this in terms of per-hour pay, a new college graduate would have to be making $33.46/hour in order to be broke!

Notice what is NOT on this list! We did not list any clothes; I hope you live someplace warm. We didn't list furniture, so you are sitting on the floor. We didn't list dishes, so you are eating with your hands. No Netflix…sad. Stamps, toilet paper, a flashlight, parking tickets, or even a tulip for your window are all examples of what you cannot have if you make $70,000 a year.

Stop for a second and think about what you just read! Yes, you can get five roommates and cut that rent payment down, and, yes, you can go without

cable to save some cash, but even if we cut this list in
HALF, you still would have a practical poverty level of
$35,000 a year [...]

Now that we have discovered that the practical
poverty level for a single individual living on their
own is $70,000 (higher for most, slightly lower for
others), it should scare you half to death to realize
the average TWO-income home makes only $57,000.
Don't forget, two people would increase your practical
poverty level since there would be a higher food bill,
more insurance, a second car—and remember, at
$70,000 you can't even afford rubber bands, so how
could you ever afford to get married?! To take this a
bit further, I have a March 2021 *Seattle Times* article
on my desk showing that if you have one child, it will
cost $284,570 to raise them from birth to eighteen
years of age.[39] Sounds high? That's only about $1,300
a month! You will need more space and more food,
insurance costs will go up, and don't forget clothes
and school expenses. Thirteen hundred dollars a
month is actually cheap when you think about it! So
that puts a small family at a practical poverty level of
$101,608 ($48.85/hour), which is the practical poverty
level for a single person, the $1,300 net increase each
month for the child and $200 extra each month to
cover all expenses from having another adult in the
home.

I know what you are thinking: "NO WAY! This can't
be right. Is this right? The math makes sense, but NO
WAY! Can this be right?!"

You have just discovered one of the biggest secrets in the world! Obviously, there are those around us who have pets. They may own a rake. This means this article has to be incorrect, right? No. What it means is if people make below the practical poverty level, they are not meeting their bills, have debt, or have lessened their life experience (e.g., having three roommates).

This means that a middle-class family should be defined as starting at $101,608 a year and that is why, from a political perspective, no political party can "fix the middle class," because they are using mid-$50,000 a year figures for the middle-class bracket. Below poverty is the same as below the water line. If you take someone from $50,000 to $58,000 they are still going to drown, aren't they?!

I am fully aware that a reader's natural instinct is to fight this article in their mind. I have heard all about how you "make $30,000 and are doing just fine," and that's good for you. But don't let your ability to manage crumbs distract you from seeing the truth, and the truth is that the math above is accurate and sound. That means we need to readjust our compass in terms of how we approach our financial lives. Again, I will remind you, I didn't even begin to touch upon things such as the need to take care of an aging parent or a disabled child or to save for a down payment on a home. You can fight this article all you want, but all you need to do is take a look around and see that what we once classified as "enough" is no longer cutting it. The faster you come to that reality, the faster adjustments can be made in order to make more than "enough."

Bottom line is, if we continue to teach our children to go to school and get a job (with a starting salary under $80,000 a year), and if we continue to focus our economy on "creating jobs," we will continue to harm our children and our nation. The focal shift needs to be made toward reaching our individual potential and that is never done through employment. Wealth is unlimited and available to everyone. From political and social standpoints, we need to encourage our leaders to shift their focus as well. Instead of "creating jobs," they need to focus on creating an environment that encourages small business, which will in turn create more jobs AND more wealth.

Note: When doing the math, don't forget to tax the individual at 30 to 35 percent.

As you can see, the numbers don't lie.

This means we are teaching this system of "job = happiness" to our children and in churches around the world, only to place our children in a pit of poverty and in another's control.

If you earn income, save income, and spend income the way the world does, then I'm sorry, you are operating in the same system in which the majority of the Western world operates in your financial stewardship, at minimum, and more likely in other areas of life as well.

Digging deeper, if inflation is 8 to 10 percent and you get a 3 percent cost of living increase at work, then you are actually losing 5 percent to 7 percent of your annual income. If you retire with $200,000 in the bank at 3 percent interest, then you are losing money every year!

This is why people in their eighties today, who made a great wage of $2.32/hour in the 1960s and were told to set aside 10 percent of their income of $4,743 a year so they could have a great retirement, are now BROKE! Just think, a man with an average yearly income of $4,743 was told about the Rule of 72. He was told that he would have more than $150,000 when he retired and he would be rich.

Here we are in 2021. How rich is he? He saved for more than thirty-one years of his then-income. (I hope he would have gotten a cost-of-living increase, but as we pointed out that really doesn't change things; we also cannot plan on things like unemployment, illness, etc., so this is just to serve as an example.) That would be the same as someone today saving up $1,376,059. If thirty-one times the average annual income wasn't enough saving for the previous generation, why would you believe it will be enough for you once you reach retirement? We have convinced ourselves in ignorance that we will be able to save our way to wealth. Math does not lie; this savings process, focusing on CDs, 401ks, and IRAs, does not work. It has never worked long term, and it will never work. It is also the way of the world, so why would or should we ever expect it to?

Not to mention, less than 10 percent of income earners will actually be able to save that amount anyway, so we are looking at something with a real-life failure rate of 90 percent. If I told you there was a 90 percent chance of rain tomorrow, would you plan on playing baseball? Of course not. But while only 10 percent of income earners make enough to reach retirement age with any amount of substantial savings, we are gladly throwing our children into a 90-percent failure-rate pond and telling them to work hard.

Employment *will always* be behind inflation. There is no way that it could have any other outcome. Even if you have the world's best boss, and we ignore how damaging employment is to every other area of your life, your boss cannot sustain 10 percent raises at work every year. It is just not going to happen, nor could it. We also saw earlier in the book how when we have long-term employment, it destroys most families and our purpose goes largely unfulfilled.

So What Do We Do?

So now that we know employment is not the answer, despite the push by the world and its "economic experts" for a job-based economy, what do we do about it? Let's examine the following parable in Matthew 25:14–30:

For the kingdom of heaven is as a man travelling into a far country, who called his own servants and delivered unto them his goods.

And unto one he gave five talents, to another two, and to another one; to every man according to his several ability; and straightway took his journey.

Then he that had received the five talents went and traded with the same, and made them other five talents.

And likewise he that had received two, he also gained other two.

But he that had received one went and digged in the earth, and hid his lord's money.

After a long time the lord of those servants cometh, and reckoneth with them.

And so he that had received five talents came and brought other five talents, saying, Lord, thou deliveredst unto me five talents: behold, I have gained beside them five talents more.

His lord said unto him, Well done, thou good and faithful servant: thou hast been faithful over a few things, I will make thee ruler over many things: enter thou into the joy of thy lord.

He also that had received two talents came and said, Lord, thou deliveredst unto me two talents: behold, I have gained two other talents beside them.

His lord said unto him, Well done, good and faithful servant; thou hast been faithful over a few things, I will make thee ruler over many things: enter thou into the joy of thy lord.

Then he which had received the one talent
came and said, Lord, I knew thee that thou art an
hard man, reaping where thou hast not sown, and
gathering where thou hast not strawed:

And I was afraid, and went and hid thy talent in the
earth: lo, there thou hast that is thine.

His lord answered and said unto him, Thou wicked
and slothful servant, thou knewest that I reap where I
sowed not, and gather where I have not strawed:

Thou oughtest therefore to have put my money to
the exchangers, and then at my coming I should have
received mine own with usury.

Take therefore the talent from him, and give it unto
him which hath ten talents.

For unto every one that hath shall be given, and
he shall have abundance: but from him that hath not
shall be taken away even that which he hath.

And cast ye the unprofitable servant into outer
darkness: there shall be weeping and gnashing of
teeth.

When we know that employment costs us in so many
areas in our lives and that financially we are guaranteed
to go backward, we are worse than all three of the mentioned men. What would be the fate of a man who said,
"Master, I was too scared to walk by faith so not only did
I bury mine, I purposely let rust and worms eat away
at it. I knew I would lose some, but everyone else was
doing it, and at best I had a little piece left by the time

you came back. Oh, I also paid rent for the land in which I buried it."

Look, I know this can be painful, and I know that parable is to teach on a Heavenly reality, but the Messiah taught a Heavenly reality using a worldly situation that the people listening (and reading thousands of year later) would understand as a stupid thing to do!

The pain that this chapter brings is not intended to harm. Rather, that pain is the feeling of lies leaving your mind. You need to stop making excuses in an attempt to make yourself feel right and justified. In reality, if you grab a calculator, your pay stub, and the Bible, you know what you have read so far is spot on.

In contrast to the pain that employment brings our way, let me paint the following picture, which I have used in other writings and presentations:

With less than 1 percent of the population earning more than $250,000 a year, I think we can all agree that that number would be widely accepted as a good income. At $250,000 a year, even if you could save every penny of that money with no expenses or taxes, how long would it take you to become a billionaire? Four thousand years! This means you would have had to start saving almost 2,000 years before the birth of the Messiah and you would just be getting there now. Keep in mind that being a billionaire in and of itself should not be a priority; I am simply using this example to expose a mathematical truth.

Why do I bring this up? Because there are now more than 1,400 billionaires on the planet that we know of. Some are worth multiple billions, like Carlos Slim Helú, who has a net worth of $82.2 billion. It would have taken Carlos 292,000 years of saving $250,000 a year to hit where he is. So what does this tell us? You cannot get rich slowly! Carlos is not 300,000 years old. The bottom line is that the only way to become wealthy is to do so quickly. I know that "getting rich quick" gives people a knee-jerk reaction of "scam," but in reality the scam is telling people they can work for $40,000 a year and become wealthy—or even have enough to live on—when they are seventy.

This is why being an Evangelpreneur is so powerful. Not because it should be everyone's goal to be a billionaire, but because it allows you to stay ahead of the world's inflationary wave! Money no longer becomes a leash around our necks that we tell ourselves doesn't really control us, nor does it matter. Instead money becomes what it was designed to be: a tool. A tool we can use to live out our purposes on earth while bringing glory to the Father. When you can stay ahead of inflation, which is only possible through business ownership, we can then start addressing the more important issues, including how to provide for ourselves, our children, and our children's children.

EVANGELPRENEUR ACTION STEP

Write down your real expenses. Before you rob Peter to pay Paul, before you put anything on a credit card, write down what really is in your life.

Looking at the practical poverty level and realizing that less than half of Americans make more than that, there are areas where we are falling behind. Where are they? Have you not bought any new clothes in five years? Are the cars nickel and diming you to death? Are you making less than 10 percent more than you did last year and the year prior?

I remember an early mentor of mine once told me that if you know within $5,000 how much you are going to make this year, you are broke, even if you are making $500,000, because it means you are not fluid, you are not expanding. Remember, when I say broke I do not mean you are just lacking money; it means you are lacking control and lacking growth. When we know how much we are going to make, within $5,000, we know that entire year we are not looking for opportunity. Heaven forbid that even people on a great pension live as though they have settled in life to the point where they no longer are growing. The statement is so true, as it leaves no room for growth or options outside what you currently have available to you.

After you've written down your real expenses, break them down by "per hour" increments. For example, if you have one child in daycare and you found a daycare that will watch your child for the bargain price of $400/week, what does that break down to? If you are working forty hours a week, $10 of every hour you work goes to child care. If your cell phone bill is $100 per month, then 63 cents of every hour goes to that bill.

We need to get away from the idea that first we'll get paid, and then we'll figure out what we need to pay with that. Once we really understand where we find ourselves, it will reveal to us where we need to go from here.

Lie of the Devil #2: It Takes a Lot of Money to Make Money

How Much Do You Really Need to Get Started?

THE LIE OF "it takes a lot money to make money" is absolutely ridiculous. The very nature of any economy proves this lie of the Devil to be false. If two cavemen started trading between themselves and the expression "takes money to make money" were true, the two cavemen would only trade the two items each had originally traded. It doesn't work that way, though. Caveman Bill could have traded a basket he made, and since the basket was used as the item of trade, it was the money. As soon as he makes another basket he has made more money. The existence of the additional basket is a benefit to everyone in the trading group, because if he traded it for another one of Caveman Joe's clubs, then Joe just increased his money and wealth as well.

If the example is true for the cavemen, then it is true for us as well. No wonder the Devil would love to keep you believing a lie that you need money to make money, because it keeps you from trying and succeeding. He doesn't want you to know the truth, for the truth shall set you free.

Here is how the lie manifests in modern times. When someone tells me they would like to start a business and I ask them what type business they would like to start, I usually get an answer along the lines of a restaurant, an exotic car manufacturer, or some other business that requires money and lots of it.

The problem isn't really that it takes a lot of money to make money; the problem for most people is they want to spend money they don't have on a business that is beyond their means. When they realize they don't have enough money to start a cupcake bakery, for example, they then spread the lie that it takes a lot of money to make money.

This is why Evangelpreneurs need to begin with what I call "starter businesses."

A starter business is a business you start with the assets and time you have available to you now. It may not be your dream business, and it can serve just as a business to raise enough money to start a larger one, but it does allow you to become an Evangelpreneur and gain control of time and money.

A few examples:

Hot Dog Cart

In the past I was a bouncer at a club, and outside three nights a week there was a vendor with a hot dog cart. I struck up many conversations with this entrepreneur and found his story to be enlightening. He used to be a professor at a local college. He wasn't happy with the low pay for the amount of hours he put in. As a way to get a bit more money, he bought this hot dog cart for a few hundred bucks from someone who had it just sitting in a barn collecting dust. He worked the cart on Thursday, Friday, and Saturday nights, the same nights that the clubs were busiest. This was back in 2000 and he was selling hot dogs for $5; for $8 you could also get a can of soda and a small bag of chips. He would head out with 300 hot dogs a night and when he sold out he was done. There was not a night I could remember that he didn't sell out, which is why he only brought 300 hot dogs. Not only did he profit more than $4 per hot dog and $6 per combo meal, everyone tipped at least a dollar. This means on the low end he was profiting $5 per hot dog, and $5 × 300 hot dogs means he took home $1,500 per night. Three nights a week equaled $4,500 in profit per week, which was $18,000 per month. Not bad for working less than 60 hours per *month*!

In his case, he gave up being a professor and spent time as a single dad raising his two sons. That was his reason, but for someone else, maybe keep your day job and put that extra $18,000 per month in a fund to buy that larger business some day.

Street Art

I was helping a business owner when one of his employees asked me about starting a business. He didn't really know what he wanted to do, but he knew he didn't want to work for someone else. His largest objection was he didn't have the money he thought he needed to start a business.

I asked him what he was good at, and he said drawing, which was true. I told him no problem, we could get him in business by the end of the week.

He would need $500 in startup money, which he didn't have. The breakdown was $75 for regulation requirements and $425 for supplies. We went to a local Italian restaurant and told them that this guy would be drawing pictures for tourists coming off cruise ships and such. If they would provide the $500, he would hand out a coupon for the Italian restaurant to everyone who purchases a picture. The restaurant thought this was wonderful because $500 for advertising was cheap, and this was even better than the typical advertising because the coupon was handed directly to a customer—a tourist who wouldn't otherwise know where to go for a meal.

The last time I heard from this guy, he was making more than $75,000 a year doing street art, working four days a week, and taking vacation whenever he wanted.

Gas Station Cleaner

This was an idea I freely gave over the air and more than one listener has now became an Evangelpreneur using it. It is simple: Gas stations know they lose money if their restrooms are dirty. The problem is that most gas stations only have one or two people working them and they cannot give up their time at the counter, stocking shelves, or servicing customers to take time away and clean the restrooms—a condition we are all familiar with.

When the smaller stations lose customers to the bigger stations because the restrooms are dirty, it really hits the bottom line.

The business plan goes something like this. With $100 you make your business legal, and with $50 you get your supplies. You then go to gas stations and offer to clean their restrooms for $30.

If you had twenty customers at twice-a-week stops, that is $1,200 extra income per week! Not bad for a business that takes less than $200 to start. As a starter business it can generate revenue for the next business effort, or you could choose to grow the business and pay another person to clean at $10 per restroom (average $20 per hour), while pocketing $20 for each restroom while you go get another 20 customers. Now the starter business could easily be putting $2,000 in your pocket each week. That is more than $100,000 per year!

Since the first edition of this book came out, I have met so many people who have used these examples (and many more we provide at our live events) and made massive amounts of money. I gave this gas station example to a man at a live event I did in Dallas; one year later he came to the event again and told me he had made over $250,000 in take-home pay after paying his staff $30 an hour, and he was only working twelve hours a week himself.

When you become an Evangelpreneur by using a starter business, you resist the lie of the Devil.

"Resist the devil, and he will flee from you." —James 4:7

EVANGELPRENEUR ACTION STEP

Over the next three days, think of ten starter businesses you could begin at this point in time. Make sure they fuel your vertical alignment (see chapter twelve) and fall into your opportunity basket (see chapter fourteen).

Note that just because a business goes into the opportunity bucket doesn't mean it also belongs on your starter business list. This list should be businesses you can start a week or two from right now with what you have available to you.

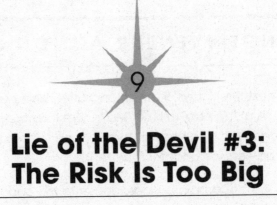

9

Lie of the Devil #3: The Risk Is Too Big

Is It Risk or Fear That Has Stopped You?

THE DEVIL HAS A HABIT of mixing a little bit of truth with a lie in order to make the lie believable. That is exactly what he did with the third lie we are going to look at.

I hear a lot of, "Josh, my wife and I would love to become Evangelpreneurs and spread our faith through the marketplace ministry, but starting a business is just too risky."

The little bit of truth is that there is risk. Of course there is risk. There is risk when you travel down the highway at 55 mph and another car is going 55 mph with literally only two feet of yellow stripe between you. Between 2001 and 2011 there were 393,696 auto-related fatalities. Yeah, driving sounds pretty risky to me. Compared to driving on the highway, how risky is starting a business?

The last time you flew, did you ask where the pilot went to flight school? Did you talk to her to make sure she wasn't drinking? A study cited in *USA Today* showed that "nearly a dozen" pilots were arrested every year from 1997 to 2009 for being drunk and attempting to fly.[40] Keep in mind that they only catch them by chance and random testing. How many are really drunk, under the influence, or sleeping while flying the plane? Nobody really knows. Yet you put you and your family on the plane without even really checking to see if a pilot is in the cockpit. That seems pretty risky.

We could list thousands of risks like these. For example, buying food from a large supermarket to feed to your children. As I write this, more than nine million pounds of beef are being recalled because for over a year now the processor knowingly had been sending out meat from diseased and contaminated cows.[41] Yet while purchasing beef, you just check the price and put it in the cart.

How risky is sending your children to school? A February 8, 2012, article in *Slate* estimated that 4.5 million children between kindergarten and twelfth grade that year have suffered some form of sexual abuse *by an educator* at some point in their scholastic career![42] FOUR AND A HALF MILLION! Yet you still send your kids to school. Is it worth the risk? (A side note: If 4.5 million kids were sexually assaulted at McDonald's there wouldn't be a McDonald's open in this country.)

We accept the risk of driving, the risk of flying, the risk of buying meat, and even the risk to our children. The problem with starting a business really isn't the risk, is it? But because many of us have been told that starting a business is just too risky, let's look at what might possibly be at risk:

- Loss of security we have from our jobs

- Money

- Failure

- Strained relationships because of too much/little time

That is it. Our lives are not at risk; our relationship with God is not at risk. So is this fear of risk justified? Of course not. It is understandable why the fear is there, and we need to look before we leap (later chapters will cover the *how* of Evangelpreneurship)—but this fear is not a game-stopper. Not only is this fear not something that should stop us based on its merits, or lack thereof, but we are told in 2 Timothy 1:7 *"For God hath not given us the spirit of fear; but of power, and of love, and of a sound mind."*

Let us examine this list of risks one by one.

Security

Your job gives you all the time off you need, pays you more than you could ever give to those in need, and everyone there shares your faith, right?

It doesn't? They don't? Hmm, that's odd.

The retirement plan is what it is all about anyway, right? I don't know if you have been paying attention over the past few decades, but nobody can count on a company or government retirement plan anymore. From military personnel to city planners, from autoworkers to pilots, the "system" has proved unreliable for just about any employee. As a matter of fact, trusting in a retirement plan is too large a risk, even for someone who loves to take risks like myself.

Retirement, for nine out of ten Americans, isn't really in the future. Seventy-one percent of people surveyed in a Wells Fargo study plans on working until eighty years old—or until they die.[43]

Maybe retirement isn't really what you should be viewing as security. The paycheck, the constant stream of income, is what you are really relying on. That is where the security really lies after all, right?

If your boss drives the company into the ground, do you have control over that? If technology or competition puts the company you work for out of business, that is in your control, too, right? When the economy warrants downsizing or when someone younger can do your job better or cheaper, that is also in your control, correct?

The answer to all of these questions is absolutely not. How risky is it to have 100 percent of your revenue-generating efforts in the hands of someone else and no control in your own hands?

How risky is it to have 100 percent of your revenue-generating efforts in the hands of someone else and no control in your own hands?

Go beyond that, though. Is the job really "working" anyway? When less than 1 percent of the population has control over time and money, there is a 99 percent chance that employment is actually not working. You know this is true, so don't let pride stop you from being honest with yourself.

Money

The second risk, which is closely related to security, is money. However, by becoming an Evangelpreneur, you're not forgoing a paycheck, you're working a different way for a livelihood. By the time you finish this book you will know what an opportunity basket is (see chapter fourteen), as well as how to identify a business that lines up with your values and objectives. We have also already covered the strategy behind a starter business, allowing you to begin a business with whatever you have available to you in terms of resources. Many starter businesses also only require part-time effort. You don't need to risk the paycheck your job offers you until it doesn't make sense for you to be there anymore. At this point this risk shouldn't be a factor holding you back.

> (W)e should be willing to risk greatly in order to strive for what we desire.

Failure

Third, there's the risk of failure. Fear of failure is a huge stumbling block. For far too long there has been a phrase going through the faith and business communities that goes like this:

"If you knew you couldn't fail, what would you do?"

The phrase is intended to get people fired up and moving toward their goals. However, the opposite effect of not moving toward your goal is actually the result, because when someone asks you this question, it automatically creates a mental block in you, suggesting that only if you knew you couldn't fail would you attempt to do these things that you value so much. But would you?

The truth of the matter is that we should be willing to risk greatly in order to strive for what we desire. Could we fail? Of course. Will we fail? Probably one or twice. When we are children, we are told that if we fail or don't succeed we should try and try again, dust ourselves off, and get back on that horse. Somehow, when we reach adulthood, failure almost has a crimson mark that comes with it. We are so afraid to fail as adults that we often fail to even try, and we motivate (or supposedly motivate) ourselves by asking absurd questions like, "If you knew you couldn't fail, what would you do?"

What is failure? As I write this I am sitting on a white-sand beach in the Caribbean with my toes literally in the water. Two miles behind me is a man raising his family on the island. Upon our meeting yesterday, he told me his story. He has two children and a wife. The wife stays home and educates the children since there is no "free" schooling here. The family eats the freshest meat, fish, fruits, and vegetables that you can imagine since they are abundant and free, or at least most of them are. He runs a business four days a week, which his oldest son helps with from time to time now that he is older. They shut down the business at 5 P.M. to make sure they don't overwork. He attends a local church and leads his family in prayer and devotions. They spend time together with other family members and friends. This is succeeding! Oh, by the way, he lives in a three-bedroom home (a little rough around the edges but a home nonetheless) and makes $100 to $150 a week. Is he still succeeding?

Of course he is, because he has control of his time and money, allowing him and his family to live out their vertical alignment (defined in chapter twelve).

Staying at the same resort as I am, there is a man who is taking a vacation because his doctor suggested it. He works for a metals company, makes six figures, and has multiple cars, but he is constantly fighting with his wife, even here, when they're on vacation. His daughter no longer talks to him, and he works more than fifty hours a week, which is ruining his relationships and his health. I kid you not, I asked him if he ever thought of getting off the corporate ladder, to which his response was, you guessed it: "That is too risky."

So, between the metals executive and beach dweller, who is the failure and who is the success?

Part of the problem with our fear of failure is that we don't really know what success is, or what it should be. If you don't know what success looks like for you and your family, then how will you know if that success is worth the risk, or have a proper understanding as to what that risk really looks like?

Relationships

The fourth most common risk I hear concerning the risks of starting a business is the risk to relationships. The idea of becoming an Evangelpreneur may be appealing, but you may feel it would strain your relationship with your spouse, parents, kids, or what have you. Your fear is that strain will be caused by either too much time together, causing the cabin fever effect (fighting and pain), or too much time apart. There could also be pressure on a relationship because of one person being the boss over another or financial ties.

If done properly, Evangelpreneurship empowers and deepens relationships—it does not destroy them. Could there be a struggle or growing pains? Yes, there could be. Would you tell your child to quit a team because his friend was named captain and he wasn't? Of course not. Should you be more mature than your children? Of course.

Regarding too little or too much time together: If Evangelpreneurship is done right according to your vertical alignment and proper business selection, time should not be a problem, as your time will be invested in people and actions that bring you closer to what is important to you and the actions that provide the most reward for the smallest time investment. When you use the starter business and opportunity basket, it eliminates the financial ties that strain relationships through having to borrow money.

This leaves the most common factor of risk to relationships, which is the boss factor. If family and friends are going to work together, the framework of leadership needs to be laid out first. It is a natural reaction for people who are close to each other to want to be equals. This reaction usually destroys businesses and relationships. As honorable as being "equal" may seem, there comes a point where a snake with multiple heads starts to eat itself, because its leadership is too divided to move forward.

That is not to say that pay cannot be equal or that people cannot have shared responsibilities. You should clarify organizational structure when working with friends or family before the business opens! Someone has to be the boss, and the others need to know their defined roles and expectations.

However, you can get creative with the boss structure to ensure equality. For example, let's assume five family members are going to go into business together and everyone wants to be equal. A chairman, who the family members unanimously agree would be the best choice to lead the whole, can be appointed. Then, there can be goals and objectives set by the group, which stipulate that if the goals and objectives are not met, then the family can revote to appoint a new chairman. The bottom line is that the roles need to be defined and the hierarchy outlined prior to opening the business.

The roles that are outlined in the business only apply to the business. For example, let's imagine that a wife and husband are working together. If the wife is the boss of the business and the husband is the head of the household, then when the business closes at the end of the workday, the roles need to be switched. This is not easy, and as a matter of fact can actually be extremely hard at first. But, if the marriage, the business, and the shared vertical alignment are important, then effort needs to be placed on the respect of each person's role. A great example of this is a past guest on my show, Christian musician Sara Groves, whose husband is her manager.[44]

With these proper understandings of this particular lie of the Devil and the truths presented here, you no longer need to fear risk.

EVANGELPRENEUR ACTION STEP

Make a list of what you want out of life. (Note that you may want to do this step again after you've done the exercise in chapter twelve about vertical alignment, because when you have your vertical alignment defined, you'll be able to see if these objectives you want to strive for in life are compatible with you achieving your alignment.)

Once you have those things listed, write down what really needs to be risked in order to achieve them. You will find that when done correctly, the risk really isn't as large as the Devil wants you to believe it is.

When you have the list of actual risks as opposed to what you previously may have perceived to be risks, take some time to decide if the risks are worth the objective.

10

Lie of the Devil #4:
You Have to Be Special

The Experience and Education You Need

T
HE LIE THAT YOU HAVE to have to be special, have certain experience, or a certain education in order to succeed is a quick lie to refute. Too often, people think that before they can become an Evangelpreneur, they need a diploma telling them that they are qualified to be a business owner. The idea that you need an MBA (or any degree at all for that matter) in order to be successful in business is simply not true. As a matter of fact, I and many other business owners view business schools and MBA programs as just places to find decent employees at best. Now, this is not to suggest that I am opposed to a college degree. If you are going to be a doctor, then yes, before you cut me open I want you to learn how to do it. Business is different, though.

Success in business is largely determined by
your ability to bring a product or service to
the marketplace in a different way than has
been done before.

Success in business is largely determined by your
ability to bring a product or service to the marketplace
in a different way than has been done before. College,
because it has to be taught to many as well as graded,
only teaches what can be replicated. Replication in business leads to failure in the long term. Look at people like
Bill Gates, Mark Zuckerberg, and Steve Jobs, who are all
college dropouts. And then there's J. R. Simplot.[45]

J. R. Simplot, who had no training more formal than
an eighth-grade education, became one of the wealthiest
people in the world. At the tender age of fourteen, this
young man started using entrepreneurial skills to think
strategically. He understood the opportunities available
in food production as the world faced economic hard
times. When the "experts" were telling people that it was
the wrong time to start a business and that it was time to
sell, J. R. knew better. He knew that people will always
need food and that the economy moves in waves. If the
price of land, product, and equipment was low because
of the economic downturn, then it was actually time to
buy. By World War II this young man had become the

largest shipper of fresh potatoes in the entire United States. In 1967 he negotiated a deal with a man named Ray Kroc, who owned a company called McDonald's. The deal made Simplot the main supplier of French fries to this new franchise burger joint. J. R. was smart: Up until that point, most restaurants cut the fries in their own kitchens, but J. R. could supply precut fries, which would lower restaurant labor costs and speed up production time. Restaurants would pay a premium for these things, and McDonald's shared his vision of precut fries. At the time of Simplot's death in 2008, he had amassed a fortune of $3.6 billion. So profound was J. R.'s entrepreneurial action that I almost titled my first book *Potatoes vs. Ivy*, a title that revealed how the entrepreneurial skills of a fourteen-year-old went against the expert advice given by Ivy League economic professors on how to navigate through the Great Depression. The fourteen-year-old won that contest hands down.

Is Higher Education Mandatory?

In 2001, Utah State University awarded Mr. Simplot an honorary degree for his many contributions to the agriculture industry in the United States. This is interesting to me, because when it comes to higher education and business, business schools only teach what other people have gone out in the real world and done. After J. R. Simplot became successful with potatoes, colleges started teaching students about his entrepreneurial actions. After Bill Gates became successful with Microsoft, colleges started teaching what he did in terms of innovation and business structure. After Mark Zuckerberg became successful with Facebook, colleges taught how he became successful in the new industry of social media. Success in business is doing what nobody else has done, but schooling is based on the foundation of replicating results, mass grading, and creating consistent systems that are applicable to many. If it were an equation, we would see that going to school for business and expecting to have success in business based on that schooling would not logically make sense.

Get Wisdom

Though I don't think it's necessary to have an MBA or even a college degree to launch a business, I am also opposed to people just starting a business and thinking they have everything they need to succeed. All three of those future businessmen who dropped out of college— Gates, Zuckerman, and Jobs—brought in experts along the way to train them. For example, Steve Jobs started Apple Inc., one of the largest companies in the world, but he knew from the beginning that he needed to surround himself with other creative experts.

Today, too many small business owners (with or without a college degree) start a business and think that the act of starting the business is all they need to be successful. If you are not constantly spending time and money in training yourself and your employees regarding marketing, advertising, branding, leadership, and about a dozen other areas of business, including sales, then you are risking too much for my taste. There is nothing more expensive than failure.

It is alarming to me that a business owner will spend $1,500 on custom cups or $4,000 on custom carpet, but when asked how much they spend on training and seminars, they'll reply, "Oh, I don't need that." Really? General Electric and Pepsi, companies that make billions per quarter, spend millions on training and seminars.

Why does the little guy who spent $80,000 on a degree struggle when all around him the big guys, many of whom didn't even finish school, are succeeding by spending their money on training and experts? It seems pretty obvious to me.

The bottom line is that no, you don't need a certain degree or some special DNA.

The bottom line is that no, you don't need a certain degree or some special DNA. You need the wisdom to know you need more wisdom. You also need a proper vertical alignment, the right motivation, and to find your opportunity baskets, which I'll discuss in chapters twelve, thirteen, and fourteen, respectively.

EVANGELPRENEUR ACTION STEP

Attend one of the seminars I conduct: Small Business—Big Solutions, Fix Your Franchise, or some other training regarding business and life success.

Create a list of skills and talents you have that those who you believe are successful do not have. Do not limit the list to what you consider to be "business skills," but rather any skill or talent you have, even personality qualities, which are not present in those you believe to be successful.

People have a tendency to compare their weaknesses to other people's strengths. This, of course, is where the biggest gap is. When we take inventory of our strengths and then compare those to what others don't have, we see we are better equipped than we have allowed ourselves to believe.

Lie of the Devil #5: Don't Mix Beliefs with Business

There Is a Belief That Beliefs Shouldn't Be in Business

COMMON ADVICE in business is not to mix business with politics or faith. So famous is this advice that it is given to more than just businesspeople. Every Thanksgiving there will be an "expert" on television talking about the holiday season and how to make sure everything goes smoothly. These experts, year after year, remind people that when sitting down to that Thanksgiving, Chanukah, or Christmas meal we should avoid talking about politics, religion, and money:

Politics: how people interact as societies, cultures, and nations internally and with other social entities.

Religion/Faith: who we are, where we came from, who created us, and where we are going.

Money: the system of exchange that empowers individuals and groups of people to accomplish tasks.

Instead of talking about these things and how they relate to our family and friends, we are told to talk instead about sports, entertainment, or our problems without desiring a solution—for talking about solutions seems to be socially unacceptable, too intimate, or too hard to accomplish, so why bother.

Yeah, that makes sense.

Would it be God or the Devil who would hope that you do not talk to the most important people in your life about the most important topics? The Devil, of course.

Integrating Values at Work

The Devil's cunning is seen in business, because millions of business owners are constantly reminded not to mix politics, faith, and other social issues with their business. The reason given is that it has no place and it just alienates segments of the customer base, which would not be good for business.

First, that is not true. Second, even if it were true, as an Evangelpreneur, someone who puts their relationship with God as a priority, it doesn't matter if it were true or not, good business or not. You are to live your life by faith and be unashamed of your faith.

Let's look at why it is not true that by giving an example of a belief and how working that belief into your business would supposedly be bad for business.

Huggies Diapers: It's a Baby!

Huggies Diapers boldly made a pro-life commercial. The ad features a man who is told by his wife that he would soon be a father. The man looks at his wife, puts a hand on her tummy, and says, "You are going to be a mom, there is a baby in there. There is a human being growing in your stomach."

This commercial instantly caught the attention of pro-life advocates, who now are loyal customers *and* promoters of Huggies. Yes, the pro-choice side didn't like that the commercial called the baby a baby, but Huggies wasn't after the market share that advocates ease of access to abortions because those people don't tend to need diapers. Diapers are for non-aborted babies.

It would be easy to say that with an industry like diapers, this example makes sense. But what about other businesses in broader product categories or service industries? The same holds true.

Chick-fil-A: Owner Didn't Chicken Out on Stating His Beliefs

When the owner of Chick-fil-A stated his belief about homosexual marriage, the "experts" were saying it would be the end of Chick-fil-A. Rallies promoted by the media and "offended" customers filled the airwaves. Meanwhile, lines of paying customers were filling Chick-fil-A stores. There were even homosexuals making a point to purchase from and support Chick-fil-A because they believed the founder should have the freedom to state his personal beliefs.[46] Chick-fil-A is big on family, and it closes its stores on Sunday so people can keep the Sabbath and spend time with family. The company, while living out the founder's beliefs, has enjoyed tremendous growth.

Hobby Lobby: We Won't Pay for Your Abortion

Hobby Lobby is another example. The company stated that it would close all its stores if it was forced into paying for certain contraception known as abortifacients through the insurance mandate. Because of the owners' desire to stand for what they believe in, their business is growing. People from around the country realized it should be acceptable for people to have beliefs and be in business. When it appeared that Hobby Lobby would be forced to either shut down or give up the values the owners held sacred, the public flocked to support them. Supporters knew that if it could happen to Hobby Lobby it could happen to all of us. Because of the increased public support, they are opening more stores to meet growing demand.[47]

Domino's Pizza: Using Its Dough to Help Others

Another example is Domino's Pizza, whose founder, Tom Monaghan, is building an entire city in Florida called Ave Maria. Monaghan is proudly professing his Catholic faith by using his business success to develop a community where like-minded people can come and live out their faith in unity. Complete with a university, homes, and retail opportunities, Monaghan's vision is clear. More importantly to our conversation is that Monaghan is not ashamed of either his business success or his religious commitments. In a world where we are told to not mix our business with our faith, this is a stark example of doing just the opposite and finding that it aids in success. As a non-Catholic, have you ever *not* bought a pizza from Dominos because of Tom Monaghan's faith? No, of course not. As a Catholic have you ever purchased a pizza from Dominos *because* of Tom Monaghan's faith? The answer is actually yes when it comes to many Catholics; the ones I asked said they love to support someone who shares their belief.

These businesses are not alone. *Duck Dynasty*, New Balance Shoes, Progressive Insurance, and many other companies have made decisions to not hide their beliefs and are reaping the financial rewards. One individual, Farris Wilks, takes being an Evangelpreneur to a whole other level. He is not only one of the wealthiest people in the nation, with a net worth of $1.4 billion, but he also is a pastor, yes pastor, of Assembly of Yahweh (7th Day) church. He understands business, he understands priorities, and most importantly, he understands YHVH's Word and how to live it! (You can hear his teachings at www.halleluyah.org.)

Values Give Your Business Value

Billions of dollars are spent every year on marketing, advertising, and branding in order to obtain and keep customers. One of the main reasons that gaining and keeping customers is so expensive is because the customer doesn't feel any loyalty toward companies. There is no reason for loyalty; price and quality change so often that everyone in business is seeking a solution.

When you mix beliefs with your business you tell the customer base that you are not one of the thousands of soulless companies after their money, but rather, you are like the customers themselves. The customer has values, beliefs, and emotions. You connect with them when you express the fact that you also have beliefs. Businesses are finding that connecting with a customer at that level creates loyalty.

Will your open display of your values keep some people from becoming customers? Sure, but there is no guarantee that they would have become customers anyway. You will also create customers who show their support by purchasing again and again and promoting your business through word of mouth. The net gain from this is much better than the "possible" reduction from those who decide not to become customers.

In addition, what you will find more often than not is that people who don't necessarily agree with your point of view will still become customers and supporters after you mix your beliefs with your business because they support your standing for what you believe. Clear stance on faith is something they don't see in the media, the government, or your competition.

EVANGELPRENEUR ACTION STEP

What beliefs or areas of life are important to you?

As an Evangelpreneur you understand that all of life mixes together, and this is wonderful, but there could be certain issues you want to use your platform to support. What are they?

Take a moment and list five issues that you would publicly stand up for. Once you have that list, for each item list another five ways standing up would manifest itself.

For example:

Pro-Life
- A. Donate product or service to pro-life charity.
- B. Have the business serve as a starting/ending point for pro-life walk.
- C. Use influence as business owner to meet with the city alderman and lobby for life.
- D. Speak at events.
- E. Post in your business resources for women who have had abortions to turn to in order to accept forgiveness and heal the pain.

PART 3

Doing Business

Step 1:
Your Vertical Alignment

Putting Your Priorities in Order

Y OU'VE STUCK WITH ME this far and have learned that in order to fulfill God's purpose for your life, you need to be the master of your finances, not have them be the master over you. You've seen the half-truths and full-on lies of the enemy and you're ready to take the steps necessary to be an Evangelpreneur. This section is for you.

It starts with ducks.

When I speak at events or do a book signing, people tell me all the time that they are going to do "x" as soon as they get their ducks in a row. They will start a business, add a new product line, get married, or have a baby when they get their ducks in a row.

I heard this so often that I started asking people what their ducks were, and to my surprise, most people have no clue. The obvious problem with that: If you don't know what your ducks are, how do you get them in a row? How do you know whether they are already in a row if you don't know what they are?

If you don't know what your ducks are,
how do you get them in a row?

I am currently working on another book tentatively titled *Who Shot My Duck: The Definitive Work on Finally Getting Your Ducks in a Row*, which addresses this issue in depth. However, I will bring up one important part of that topic now, because it is so vital we get this issue figured out and implemented correctly in our lives.

What Is Vertical Alignment?

One of the major teaching points I cover is getting things lined up and moving (that is, getting those ducks in a row)—vertical alignment.

Vertical alignment is sometimes touched upon in a church setting, but even then there is a tendency not to teach it, but rather merely mention it and make some vague suggestions. Most people don't even know what a vertical alignment is, let alone have one.

A vertical alignment is the order in which you place things in your life. For example, a common alignment may look like this:

1. Faith
2. Spouse
3. Children
4. Country
5. Work
6. In-laws/extended family

Your list may be longer and could be in a completely different order, or depending on the different seasons and circumstances of life. For example, a single person wouldn't have "spouse" on his or her list. Determining the things that are important to you and the order of their importance is paramount to achieving success in all areas of life. This step affects your business as much

---

Determining the things that are important
to you and the order of their importance is
paramount to achieving success
in all areas of life.

as it affects your marriage; it affects your entertainment choices as much as it affects your eating habits.

When we fail to have a vertical alignment, success can become a curse. How many politicians (regardless of political party) have been caught in sex scandals? How many celebrities have millions of dollars, yet go to rehab as often as most of us get our oil changed? How many professional athletes have an undeniable drive to succeed, yet blow through their tens of millions in only a few short years after they retire? These examples show how fame and money themselves cannot order your life. You need to place them in a correct framework, as in a good vertical alignment.

Let me point out that we have all sinned and fallen short of the glory of God, and we are all made white as snow by the blood of the Messiah if the gift of Christ's sacrifice is accepted and our repentance is true. With that said, we are facing the reality that disaster comes from not living out the proper vertical alignment.

The Military's Ducks

When someone is in the Army, they say they are "in the Army"; when someone is in the Navy, they say they are "in the Navy"; and when someone is in the Air Force, they say they are "in the Air Force." This trend does not continue to the Marines, though. When someone is in the Marine Corps, they do not say they are "in the Marines"—they say they *are* a Marine. Their service becomes part of their identity, and it never goes away. Once a Marine, always a Marine. This is why you have ninety-two-year-old men cruising around nursing homes with "Semper Fi" bumper stickers on their electric wheelchairs.

The Marine Corps is also the only branch that integrates a vertical alignment as a part of their structure and identity. That is why they ARE Marines as opposed to being *in* the Marines. When you live out your vertical alignment, it becomes who you are. There is debate within the Marines as to whether their vertical alignment is ordered "God, Country, Corps," or "God, Corps, Country," as Commander Ernest Passero used in his article "For God, Corps, and Country"[48]—but it seems that the latter is more evident in the lives of the Marines I have met, so let's use that one for our teaching purposes:

1. God
2. Corps
3. Country

You may be wondering why they would put "Corps" before "Country." You may also question "God" being first, because atheists can serve, too. Furthermore, should "God" even be on the list?

The reason the Marines put God first is because that is where they get their sense of values. Don't kill needlessly, don't pillage a village, et cetera. If "God" comes after "Corps" or "Country," a Marine could decide to take land unjustifiably or rape a woman in a village (because Godly values would no longer be the pillar supporting all other decisions). You may say, "But that does happen, and Marines have been found guilty of terrible crimes against the innocent." This is true, but that is because those service members didn't live out the Marines' vertical alignment. When people do not have and live out a vertical alignment, all sorts of problems follow.

When people do not have
and live out a vertical alignment,
all sorts of problems follow.

"God" is first, and then comes "Corps." The reason "Corps" comes next is because the unit of men and women has your life in their hands and puts their lives in yours. Marines even joke that when Marines die, they go to Hell to regroup. Now, I would pray that they go the other direction, but the point is that they carry their identity and unit loyalty even after death. If the United States were to fall from an external or internal threat (the latter seems more likely) and the "country" decided to split up or become part of a foreign nation, the Marine Corps has made the commitment to remain a unified fighting unit.

They are only able to protect the country so well because they have made this commitment to each other above their country.

Then comes "Country." Now, before a reader makes the mistake of thinking that country is not important to a Marine, let me clarify. It is because they love their country and because they have it in the proper place on the vertical alignment that allows them to serve their nation with all that they have.

Look at vertical alignment like this: When you place priorities in the correct order and fully live them out, it allows you to take what is lower on the list and elevate it. In the case of the Marines, the country is last, but because of how they live out their alignment, the last is lifted up, because they serve their nation in a way other units cannot.

Our Forefathers' Ducks

Our founding fathers had a vertical alignment. Today's generation believes that the founding fathers placed patriotism above their nation, which is an example of how we often misunderstand vertical alignment. They were patriotic, and they understood that there is no greater love than to lay down your life for your brother. However, the United States of America was not the priority. As a matter of fact, would you believe that the United States didn't even rank in their top five priorities?

For most of them, God came first. This was followed by their spouse. After their wives came their children. Next came the ability to own their own lives and not be servant to the Crown. Entrepreneurship (which includes land ownership) was next. This is why some of the symbolism used on flags and banners represented business interests, such as the pine tree on Maine's flag, and why taxing a product like tea, without fair representation back in England, initiated a revolution.

Because these men lived out their vertical alignment so well, we assume the nation they founded was their priority. In reality, they knew that they needed to create a nation that protected these concepts:

1. God
2. Spouse
3. Children
4. Owning their own lives
5. Entrepreneurship

The founders knew that a mighty nation would need to exist in order for them to realize their priorities. They had such a passion to live out their priorities that they were willing to lay down their lives in order to even have a chance of making this nation—a nation that allowed the freedom needed to live out their priorities—a reality. As a result, they changed the entire world.

What Are Your Ducks?

How do we determine the right order for our vertical alignment? That is up to you, and it is not easy. This is going to take some time to work out, and your vertical alignment may not be like your neighbor's or friend's.

When creating your list, it is common for parents to put children in the number-two spot. I cannot tell you how to place items on your list, but let me give you an example as to why this may not be the wisest choice.

A gentleman I know, who also talks a bit about this particular issue, places his wife second. He makes sure he serves her, cherishes her, and is her hero. He makes a point of ensuring she knows she is loved, protected, and is second in his life only to God. There was a point during the holiday season where someone asked, "Why do you spoil your wife with gifts and you don't spoil your children?" (Let me be sure to acknowledge that he is a great father, and he spends tons of time loving and raising his children. He also gives them nice gifts; I am referring here to materially spoiling his wife.)

His answer was wonderful. He told the person questioning his action that he and his wife were joined together by God and will spend forty to fifty years together. His children will spend only five more years in the home and then they will move and get married. "I want my daughter to want a man who will treat her for the next fifty years the way I treat her mother, and I want my sons to see how a man treats a woman." By placing his children below his wife on his list, he showed them a better life value than if he treated his wife like his "old ball and chain" and spoiled the kids.

What about yourself? Where do you place yourself on your list? Should you be at the top? I would suggest no, but it is up to you. Should you be at the bottom? No, I think you should find yourself more important than home maintenance, for example. So we need to think about where we place ourselves. The great thing about the way God created vertical alignments is that whatever is lower is still served as the more important things are lived out. Wanting some physical love from your spouse is not bad, but it should not be the main goal. When giving him or her love is the focus, then you are more apt to get (and be happy with) the physical love you want. The same is true with other desires.

When deciding how to position each item on your vertical alignment, you need to ask yourself:

- Why is this item important to me?
- What is less important to me than this?
- What is more important to me than this?
- Is this really that important at all?

The last question is the one that can make the process of determining the order of your alignment much easier.

If "softball team" is one of the things for which you are trying to figure out a place, ask yourself if it is important at all. The answer may be an easy "no" because we have been conditioned to say that. Granted, we don't really develop a purposeful vertical alignment by including it. We all seem to know that a hobby shouldn't be a priority. But if you are spending $100 on a bat, $150 on cleats, and three nights a week away from home, is it really a "no"? Your investment shows it has importance to you, so it is already on your list whether you realize it or not. What you need to do is figure out its proper place on the list—or if it needs to come off the list because, in doing this process, you realize it's been too high a priority.

I am not saying you shouldn't play softball. If your health is high on the alignment list, then playing a sport could assist with this priority. If spending time with your wife and kids is high on your list, then it is good for the relationship that you have a hobby or sport like softball, because it allows you to get away from the wife and kids for a while so your batteries can recharge, which in turn will let you better serve them with patience and enthusiasm. It all comes down to where the items fall on the list, and what is getting more time compared to what is supposed to be more important. Every married person is going to say their spouse is important, just like every politician is going to say the Constitution is important. However, actions speak louder than words, so how you're spending your time and money is showing what your priorities actually are. If you write out what they are and then live according to that, you can truly live out your priorities.

When your heart is after the right things and your priorities are in the correct order, good works will manifest in your life.

"A good man out of the good treasure of his heart bringeth forth that which is good; and an evil man out of the evil treasure of his heart bringeth forth that which is evil: for of the abundance of the heart his mouth speaketh."
—*Luke 6:45*

Making Your List

Okay, brass tacks. When do we make the list?

My suggestion is to take a weekend and just get away. Don't go someplace with too many activities. I told someone to do this once and they went to Las Vegas; not exactly what I meant.

Instead, get away in a manner that removes you from distractions. If you are married, get away together. Take time to determine the things that really matter to you as individuals and as a couple. This process can take two entire days, and the list could have five items or thirty-five items. There is no way I can give you a cookie-cutter directive; each couple will have a different list of priorities. Then, if you are married, review with your spouse the lists you have made. Do not just go over each other's lists—explain why each item is of importance. Single or married, decide what you can do to live out this list every day. What actions can you live out that will advance each item, and what in your life can you change in order to get more in line with your newly formed vertical alignment? Sometimes those changes are easy, like limiting spending or taking a half hour every morning to study the Scriptures. Other decisions are tougher, such as ending relationships or relocating. Some actions as seemingly trivial as changing how you dress or what you typically do on a Friday night can cause great heartache.

Heartache tends to be common when we change our lives to line up with our vertical alignment, but the pain is temporary and necessary.

A Couples List

If you're married, then you need to make another list, this time with your spouse. While each of you will certainly have your own unique lists, as a married couple you need to develop a joint list as well. The two of you have become one flesh. A two-headed snake tends to fight against itself and has a challenge moving forward, so make sure to act with one head. Make a list of things that are your priorities as a couple. You will notice that many of the top items on the list may actually be identical to what each of you has on your individual lists, and that is great, but you must agree on what is important to you as a couple for your marriage to succeed.

You will find that successful couples, whether or not they have they believe in God, share a value system that they live out as a couple. To the surprise of believers, there are atheist couples who have more successful marriages because such couples, sometimes without even knowing they have done it, have established their vertical alignment as a couple and live it out together.

Children's Lists

Continue this trend of making vertical alignments when you get home, too. If you have children, then instruct them to make their own lists. Obviously, the list will be age reflective. Your six-year-old will have a different set of items than your sixteen-year-old, but having them write out their priorities helps get them on the right track—like you, they still will need to match their actions to their list. Also, the list gives you the opportunity to actually raise your children as opposed to just parent them until they leave the house. Raising your children involves teaching them what you want them to believe, sharing with them ways to make decisions according to your family's moral compass, purposely deciding what information they take in, and other elements that convey a desired outcome.

Today's parenting seems to be more along the lines of get them to school, feed them, become their best friend, and let them develop their own morals and beliefs without your instruction or suggestion while hoping for the best. We don't treat our pets that poorly, yet that is considered modern parenting. Taking time to talk to them about how they are living out their alignment, and sharing how you and your spouse, and the family as a whole, live theirs out, allows the family to grow as a unit and as individuals. Seeing other members of the family and the family as a whole living out what is important encourages everyone else in the family. When children make mistakes, parental corrections teach that errors are learning opportunities that allow us to improve.

When your family knows what it wants, and it works together to achieve it, you create bonds that cannot be broken.

Now, Show That You Mean It

This brings us to the key to making the whole vertical alignment effective—living it out. You have to work your vertical alignment; otherwise, it is nothing more than a list of things you think are cool.

Too often, despite what we've written down, we place ourselves at the top of the list. We tell ourselves God, our spouse, or our kids are more important, but in reality it is us that we place on top. We wake up in the morning and ask God for stuff, we kiss our spouse in hopes of getting love in return, we take our kids out in public to show off how good we are doing as parents, and we display the flag so the neighborhood knows we are patriotic. Life becomes about what we can get out of it: money, power, pleasure, praise, sex, or some other self-focused goal.

In the verse below, God talks about this importance of living out your vertical alignment *and* getting your earthly desires. The world thinks you have to sacrifice your desires if you trust in God, but in reality that is the only way to receive your desires.

"But seek ye first the kingdom of God, and his righteousness; and all these things shall be added unto you." —Matthew 6:33

God is saying that you should put Him at the top of your vertical alignment and live it out. "Seek" is an action word; it requires doing. He did not say "scribe" first. He said "seek."

Making a list (scribing) is the easy part; any kindergartener with a crayon and a writing surface can make a list. Actually, they would probably do a good job, writing a list like, "God, Mommy and Daddy, my little brother, the dog."

You need to wake up every day and make the decision to make sure your other decisions advance your list. Every decision you make, regardless of how seemingly insignificant, has an impact. After all, if sponsoring a child in Africa costs 50 cents a day, and a pack of gum costs 50 cents, the decision about whether to buy a pack of gum each day is not insignificant. It, too, becomes something that moves you closer to or further from living out your alignment and achieving your goals.

To be honest, big decisions are actually easier to handle. If you are away on business and in the lobby of a hotel, and a woman invites you to her room, it is easy to say, "No, I'm married." But if you are alone in your room, and the TV offers certain pay-per-view movies, that decision is harder. If your family moving to Chile is important to you, it is easy to say no to the new sports car. It is harder to say no to the daily mocha latte, but that five dollars every day moves you further from your goal and doesn't match your alignment if money needs to be budgeted to make the move.

Decisions are not as simple as "yes" or "no" all the time, either. You need to make sure you invest time in developing your role in each area of your list. When you invest time, you invest yourself, and when you invest yourself, your heart draws near to what it finds important.

EVANGELPRENEUR ACTION STEP

Everyone is going to have priorities like wife, kids, God, country, family, and community on their lists.

Take the time to really expand this list, because the more that is on it, the less confusion there is as to where things should be in your life. These are some of the possible items that may be on one's list:

- Job
- Entertainment
- Hobbies
- Politics
- Household maintenance
- Technology (TV, phones, computers)
- Reading
- Continued education
- Community involvement
- Travel
- Extended family
- Protecting the home
- Pets
- Food
- Appearance (hair, nails, tan, etc.)
- Health and fitness

It is not unrealistic to have a list with dozens of things, and in a way it is almost impossible to identify everything on your list right away, because you will find there are things that take up time and effort in your life you didn't even realize were there.

If you really want to get good at this, take thirty days and carry a little notepad in your pocket or purse. Every time you transition from one activity to another, write it down. Driving—Banking—Driving—Soccer Practice—Driving—Cooking. At the end of a month, you will see what you have really placed near the top of your list.

This chapter is really just step one in a much larger training I conduct entitled "Meaning of Life." I would strongly suggest you attend an event or watch the video series pertaining to this full teaching.

Writing down each transition and what you transition to truly can mean the difference between failure and success, and success and significance.

Step 2:
Identify Your *Why*

What Should Be the Reason
You Work So Hard?

N THE FAITH-AND-BUSINESS INDUSTRY, there has been a push to amplify one's *why*. Some motivational fluff out there goes as far as saying things like, "When your *why* is big enough, the 'how' doesn't matter."

Let's think about the ridiculousness of that for a minute. I get the concept; you are so motivated by why you are doing something that the process to accomplish it doesn't matter; it shouldn't stop you, and nothing is too difficult. If I was six years old and this was a fairy tale, I would be on board with this motivational statement, but reality doesn't support it.

What if your *why* was to get a new Porsche, and that was your motivation? Would it matter that you earned the $70,000 to buy the car by dealing drugs? I thought the *how* didn't matter? What if you wanted a successful business in order to provide a private education for your children, which costs $15,000 a year? You are earning that money by working for a company that is experiencing double-digit downsizing for five years straight, and requires fifty hours a week away from home. The *how* does in fact matter!

This motivational fluff is spouted to the masses by motivational speakers, because those speakers cannot teach the *how*, so they hide behind a false *why*. They are like the wizard in *The Wizard of Oz* hiding behind the curtain.

Another motivational line that is essentially useless beyond the motivational moment of excitement it provides is, "When you want to succeed as bad as you want to breathe, then you will be successful."

Would you dare say this around someone who lost a loved one to drowning? Did the deceased not want it bad enough? Did they just not try hard enough to succeed? I get it, it makes for a great poster in the gym. However, if that sort of fluff is the type of words you use to live by, you will fail! If you really need words to live by, may I suggest: *"But he answered and said, It is written, Man shall not live by bread alone, but by every word that proceedeth out of the mouth of God."* —Matthew 4:4

With all that being said, and with most motivational speakers mad at me by this point because I just let the air out of their balloon, let me say that your *why* is extreme-ly important.

Your *why* has to be real, and the deeper the meaning in your heart and soul, the better.

Let's go back to the Porsche we used in the example. Wanting or having a Porsche is not bad in itself. If your vertical alignment is in place, then the *how* should not be a problem, either, but *why* do you want the Porsche? The Porsche is just a symbol of something else, another *why*. Perhaps the *why* is because when you first started your business, that was the image of success. Getting the Porsche is a gift to yourself, symbolizing that you did it; that is not bad.

Let's look at another example: A diamond necklace is *why* you think you are working hard, but is it really the necklace that you want? Probably not—the necklace is really your way of showing your wife that she is special to you. Yes, I know it shouldn't take a necklace to do that, but please realize these are just examples. The point is that we need to dig a bit and get to the *why* of objects we desire.

Self-Examination Time: What's Your *Why?*

While this book is going to bring many people to the conclusion that they should become an Evangelpreneur because it just makes sense from a financial and freedom prospective, that is pretty broad and applies to pretty much everyone. What you need to do now is *ask yourself why you specifically want to be an Evangelpreneur.* Why do you want to be successful? It is easy to say that you want to be a success to serve your vertical alignment, and that is 100 percent true. But we need to take that *why* and visualize it. What does it look like to you? How is the day-to-day operation going to play out? How is it going to feel emotionally to know you are in pursuit of your purpose? Who do you want to include in your pursuit? How is life going to change? Just get as detailed as possible, for when a vision is void of details, it really isn't a workable vision—it is more of a dream.

(W)hen a vision is void of details, it really isn't a workable vision—it is more of a dream.

Your *why* should integrate an element from your vertical alignment and a goal or accomplishment associated with that element.

For example, if God is on your vertical alignment and you want to serve Him, what method have you chosen to do that? Is it sending Bibles into the Congo? If so, then *why* are you working so hard this week? To send Bibles into the Congo. The Bible itself isn't the *why*; doing something with the Bible is the *why*.

A single mother working double shifts doesn't do it for the better car she is trying to buy. That is not the *why*. She is working the double shifts to buy that better car so she can take her kids to school without the fear of it constantly breaking down and therefore keeping her kids from getting to class on time. The car is the goal, but the kids are the *why*, and the kids are higher on her vertical alignment than herself or her job. She leaves work tired but feeling like she is accomplishing something for her kids.

Now, let's change the example just a little bit. A mother is working double shifts and she tells everyone her kids are important. However, instead of using that money to buy a car she buys herself new clothes and goes out with her friends every weekend. Monday morning comes, and she tells herself that spending the money partying is okay because she deserves it after working so hard. The kids having to walk to school while she takes the bus to work is just part of life at the moment. The kids grow to resent her, as they see they are not the priority.

Does the second mother deserve time to relax because she works so hard? Yes. Who is higher on her vertical alignment, her or the kids? Herself. As the kids grow, if this mother continues to put herself above the kids, she will grow further and further apart from her kids. If we asked her what her *why* is for working, you know as well as I do that she would say something like, "I work so hard for my kids at home." If we asked her to write down her vertical alignment, I bet you dollars to doughnuts that she would place her kids ahead of herself. But her actions don't line up with that.

Mini Action Step:
Map Out Your Goals/Related *Whys*

Now you try it. Take your vertical alignment, and next to each item in the top ten, write something you would like to accomplish for that item. For example, if YHVH is first on your list, perhaps something you would like to accomplish is sending a box of Bibles into North Korea or planting a church in a new region of the world.

Incidentally, it is okay to have yourself on your own vertical alignment list—although I hope that you are not near the top. So put a goal next to yourself as well. When you are working through your alignment and you have *why*s next to each one, that means you are pursuing those *why*s in the appropriate order. The alignment is the important elements in life, the *why* is *not* why the element is on the list but rather your reason for your efforts in life regarding that element. A husband has his wife on his list, his *why* regarding his wife could be to fill Scriptural command to love his wife (Ephesians 5:25). By the time you get to yourself, it is not an act of selfishness; it is an act of caring for yourself. If God cares for you, and you care for God, it would be crazy not to care for what God cares about, so you do need to have goals that are just yours, too.

Your achievement of your goals will not always line up with the effort or the list, and that is okay. When people are new to making and working a vertical alignment as well as creating a real list of *why*s, they tend to get concerned when goals aren't achieved in their exact listed order. While your top item on the alignment list may be the most important, you often seem to be hitting your *why* goals for lower items faster or more often.

This is actually to be expected. Let's say item one is God and your *why* for him is building an orphanage in Haiti. Item number ten is your softball team and your *why* goal for them is marking the baselines. Obviously, marking the baselines is achievable faster and with much less effort. That doesn't mean your softball team came first. As long as your primary focus and drive continue to line up with the alignment, you are fine; it doesn't mean you are doing anything wrong or that your alignment is "off."

Let's consider again the example of the single mom working a double shift in order to buy a new car. Had she written this out, next to "work" on her vertical alignment, what she wants to accomplish would be "make enough money to buy a new car" and the *why* next to that would be "so I can get the kids to school safely and on time." Your vertical alignment, your goals, and the *why*s you have for those goals should be so intertwined at each level that there is really no separation, because your alignment element drives your *why*s, which drives your goals.

Having this in place properly sees you through hard times and develops a servant's heart.

Be Honest

You really have to be honest with your *why*s. It could be that right now your *why*s don't match up with what you think your alignment is. This is an indication that your alignment isn't quite what you think it is. There is a great verse in Matthew that talks about how what really is important to us is where we will invest ourselves: *"For where your treasure is, there will your heart be also."* —*Matthew 6:21*

Remember that treasure is not just money. Treasure is what you value. Time, money, and beauty or your youth are a few examples of treasure, because they are things upon which we all place a value. You have treasure, and you need to do some soul searching and see where you have been placing it. Ask yourself, what do I do with my time? With my money? With beauty?

Be careful not to fall for the Christian trap of thinking that just because you go to church or have a Jesus fish on your bumper that you have your heart in the right place and your *why*s are where they should be.

I have met so many pastors, elders, and church members who are so backward in their real priorities that they are actually in a worse place than the bad mother we used as an example. The Christians who find themselves in this position have a tendency to believe they have it right, and fail to recognize or correct their actions. They hide behind words like "grace," "priorities," "mercy," or even "head of the home," and don't realize that they are to put themselves last to be first, and serve as Christ served.

EVANGELPRENEUR ACTION STEP

Your action step, besides doing what I outlined already in the chapter, is to identify what in your life is worth dying for.

When you have nothing worth dying for, you have nothing worth living for. When you have nothing worth living for, you have nothing worth fighting for. This is why so many people complain about life, yet don't do anything about it. Some of the most common complaints pertain to politics, society, broken relationships...the list goes on.

Your entire vertical alignment should be important, and there should be a *why* next to many items on your list.

I want you to take your list and literally draw a line at a certain point. This line is going to be the point that designates that everything on the list above it is worth dying for, and everything below it is not worth dying for.

For example, your list may look like this:

1. God
2. Spouse
3. Children
4. Extended Family
5. My Business

You might be thinking, "Josh, where on my list do I put 'fellow man,' because the Bible says: 'Greater love hath no man than this, that a man lay down his life for his friends' (John 15:13). But I don't have 'fellow man' on the list."

The truth is, if God is on your list, you do! Who said that there is no greater love than one who will lay down their life for another? God. If you're living your life in alignment with God's commands, doing good to your fellow man is among your priorities.

Once you have that line that determines what you are willing to die for (and ultimately want to live for), you have your purpose boundary. The founding fathers had a line, the apostles had a line, and you should have a line. While lower things on your list shift and vary due to time and circumstances, what is above your line doesn't change short of an act of God.

Step 3:
The Opportunity Basket

Figuring Out What Business
Is Right for You

REMEMBER WHEN I WAS A YOUNG KID, I had a
grandma who had a large garden with many fruits and
vegetables. I liked taking a basket down to the garden
and helping her pick something for supper. My grandma tried to teach me what a ripe tomato looked like, and
not to be fooled by one that looked almost ripe enough.
I had the hardest time telling whether the melons were
ripe. Pluck it, roll it, and smell it, she said, but I still had
the hardest time telling.

It wasn't hard to identify what the food was: a water-
melon, zucchini, or strawberry. That was easy. The hard
part was deciding if it was ready enough to put in my
basket.

I find that those who want to be small business owners often have a similar problem.

These soon-to-be small business owners make their way to the marketplace and see a business that is for sale, inspires an idea, or even serves as an example. They want a business, so they pick the one easiest to grab. Most of the time that means they end up struggling with their business months later. More often than not, they experience failure.

Just as with a garden, you don't want to pick the first plant you come across. It needs to be the kind you are looking for, and it has to be ripe.

If I had to give an estimate, I would say that well over three-quarters of the struggling or failing businesses I have seen are a direct result of the owner not only picking the wrong business, but also picking or placing that business at the wrong position within a certain industry. In other words, it wasn't ripe for the picking.

When it comes to business, what could be great for your opportunity basket may not be perfect for someone else.

In this chapter, we will look at how to determine your opportunity basket—a process to identify whether you should consider a certain type of business. A few notes first. In a garden, a non-ripe plant is not good for anyone. However, it's a little different in entrepreneurship. When it comes to business, what could be great for your opportunity basket may not be perfect for someone else. Also, just because something may go into your opportunity basket *does not* mean that you should get involved with that particular business. There are more factors to consider before you get involved other than just the fact that an opportunity is present (more on that in chapters fifteen and sixteen).

Let's start picking. The following are factors that may influence your business choices.

What You Are Good At

I am not a strong believer in the idea that just because you are good at something or have experience in a certain arena, it makes sense for you to build a business around that. As a matter of fact, choosing a business based on your past experience tends to mislead you that being good or experienced is all it takes for success. Many businesses have failed because their owners thought that their experience was the only necessary factor, from car manufacturers like DeLorean to restaurants that only rely on having a good chef. Millions of businesses have failed because their owners foolishly thought their past experience and previous success in an industry would equate to success in their own business.

For example, a plumber has obviously been employed in the plumbing industry. A plumber who starts his own plumbing business is now not only in the plumbing industry, but also in the business industry, because business itself is an industry. Being a good plumber and offering better service than the competition is not even in the top-ten list of qualities that determine success in business. Understanding profit partnerships and laddering conversations, for example, would be higher on the list.

Tens of thousands of chefs cook a better burger than McDonald's, yet tens of thousands of chefs have tried unsuccessfully to own restaurants. There are thousands of opera singers who are better at singing than Justin Bieber and Britney Spears, but how many can you name? An opera singer may be more qualified than, say, Garth Brooks, yet he or she goes to his or her job at the city opera house (i.e., works for somebody else) and makes only $60,000 a year, while Garth sold out five back-to-back shows in Ireland in minutes, pocketing more than $36.5 million on one day alone. Yet you, the opera singer, with more range, better tone, and great pitch, thought that a great voice would equal success in the entertainment industry? The reason the successful examples were successful was because they, or the team around them, knew that the most important skill set to possess and develop are business skills.

It may seem like I am opposed to someone starting a business in an industry where they have experience. Not true; my point is that you need to know that experience should not be a leading reason for choosing a business to put in your opportunity basket. Being good at something *could* certainly lead to a strategic advantage over those in the industry who do not have your experience, especially if you know things such as how the industry operates and who the major players in the field are, and I'm not saying that no experience in an area is a wise approach. But sometimes simply hobby-level expertise is enough. I have started businesses in industries where I have had experience, and there is no doubt that the prior experience was a benefit. I also have started businesses where I saw an opportunity, and with less experience than the competition, I still had success. Keep in mind that "success" in my short-term ventures usually means becoming more profitable than the competition in a very short time span. "Success" in my long-term businesses may mean developing a brand or impacting the industry for years without immediate profit, because the long-term objective is much more important and takes longer to achieve.

Placement in an Industry or Marketplace

A huge mistake I witness time and time again is placing a business in the wrong starting position.

When you go boating, most people launch their boat from a public boat launch. This creates congestion at the launch and surrounding area. If you and the other boats are involved in similar boating activities, the congestion and frustration continues, because there is not enough room for you to fully take advantage of what your boat can do. The day of boating takes a different tone if you have a friend who lives on the river, because you can use her boat launch, which, at a point away from the regular launch area, is free of any congestion.

In business that same problem could look like this. You love coffee and you think everyone loves coffee. You see Starbucks making billions, and there are fifteen other coffee shops in your town, so it must be a good market to go after, right? You start your new coffee-shop business, and as you learn more about your local industry, you find out that four of those other shops are only open because they are locked into long-term leases. Eight of them are open because they have income sources outside the coffee shops, such as a spouse's income, investment income, or even employment outside of their business. Another three are barely making enough money to keep the bills paid, and two of the fifteen are actually making a profit. But, you love coffee, saw the multiple businesses, and thought there was an opportunity.

Was there an opportunity? It is easy to laugh and say "no," as the example is statistically true in terms of profitable businesses in an industry, but the answer is actually "yes." The only difference between the given example and a good opportunity would be where you placed yourself in that industry.

What if you love coffee, you want to be in the coffee industry, but now you look at the marketplace and realize that your business could fulfill a different need than you originally thought? For example, you may discover that the two major suppliers of coffee to the fifteen local stores are all out of state and distributed from three different locations. This causes price and supply chain irregularities and problems for those fifteen local shops in town. You look at the $50,000 you allotted to start your coffee shop, and decide that instead of going the coffee-shop route you'll spend $3,000 on warehouse space in town. You invest $2,700 in some high-level business training and another $1,500 traveling to industry-supply trade shows, where you secure bulk coffee suppliers out of Colombia. You spend another $1,000 to work on packaging for your own private special blend.

You approach the fifteen local store owners and let them know you can supply them faster, more reliably, and more affordably than the out-of-state suppliers. You can supply similar coffee to what they already use, and you can also provide a special blend that those out-of-state suppliers don't even have access to.

You secure contracts with ten out of the fifteen. Your overhead is lower, you are making money on 67 percent of all coffee sold in town, you work fewer hours than the typical retail shop owners, and you have $41,800 of your start-up egg left over, so you decide to take your husband on a cruise.

Same industry, different opportunity.

There are millions of examples that show how to identify opportunities like our example—far too many to cover in this book. My suggestion is for you to attend one of my multi-day business workshops, because they dig deeper to spot those opportunities. You will become so proficient in the skill of opportunity evaluation that you will start finding opportunities everywhere.

Competitive Landscape

There are two forms of competition: direct and indirect. We will only deal with direct competition in this example as it is more applicable, but I strongly suggest you study both forms.

Most people reading this book do not have millions of dollars to start a business, which by default classifies most future Evangelpreneurs as small-business Evangelpreneurs. As such, you will most likely have a lot of direct competition. Someone with $10 million in startup funds can start a 3-D printing company for DNA-specific organ generation, and may have five direct competitors on the entire planet. Someone with $4,000 looking to start a pest control company may have sixty direct competitors in just a fifty-mile radius!

Competition does not mean that you shouldn't enter the industry; you just need to search out the opportunity.

Let's use pest control as an example.

"Case Study"—Pest Control

In your town you have the two big national names in pest control and you have twenty-five small companies. Through your research, you discover that only a certain percentage of a population base will use professional pest control. You take your population and find the number, using your percentage, of how many potential customers there are in your town. Let's say you have a town of 250,000 people, and statistically only 10 percent of the population will ever purchase the service. That means the size of the local pie is 25,000 customers. Of those 25,000 customers you will most likely see half go to the big national brands (the power of good branding), leaving only 12,500 customers for the remaining twenty-five businesses to share—or, if you jump in, twenty-six businesses. Not all client lists are going to be equal in reality, but for evaluation purposes we see that the average customer base is 480 clients per small company. Two-thirds of that client list is not going to be monthly or even yearly clients, so they are not "bankable." In other words, you cannot plan your business on these hit-or-miss customers. This leaves about 158 bankable clients per year. Of those, maybe one-half would want a monthly service call. This gives you a realistic monthly income of $3,950, using an average of $50 per service call.

Out of that $3,950, you will pay $700 for office rent, and $3,333 for the receptionist/bookkeeper/manager because you cannot run the books, answer the phones, deal with the daily worries, *and* go provide the services. Supplies will run $250 a month, $180 on the payment for your truck and equipment, and $150 a month for phone and internet. Additionally, don't forget $200 per month to pay off the loan you took out for getting your license, website, work uniforms, business cards, and decal for the truck. You have another $50 in business account fees at the bank, and $40 a month in business association dues. Since this is your income, your business income needs to pay for your personal bills, as well. At home, your monthly expenses are $750 for rent, $65 for cable, $120 for electric and water, $400 in food, and so on. Oh, don't forget gas. Between your work and your personal life, and given that you need a truck, you are looking at gas expenses of easily $400 a month. You and I both know there are many more monthly expenses, but with just what we have listed here, you are $2,688 short every month. You need to make $6,638 just to break even!

This means you would be doing about seven service calls a day just to pay the bills, and since you are working in other people's homes, you can't say you will work fourteen-hour days. Oh, and don't forget taxes, which means you actually need to do eight service calls a day, with eight out of the eight service calls each day simply going toward breaking even.

Let me make sure you understand this. Your monthly businesses expenses are $4,903 and personal expenses are $1,735. This means total expenses of $6,638 on an income of $3,950. You are losing $2,688 every month. There are additional costs like insurance, advertising, and a half-dozen other business and personal expenses I haven't even mentioned.

This little bit is by no means enough, and, unfortunately, most business owners don't even do this much research, let alone the amount necessary before launching a business. Sadly, many people think, "Hey, there are 250,000 people in my town, and so if I do eight service calls a day [one hour per service call], five days a week, I will make $2,000 a month."

The tendency for businesses to overlook these sorts of calculations is just one of the reasons why more than 83 percent of all small business owners are failing! When looking into the failure rate, I remember seeing a study that pointed to 83 percent being the statistic, which I choose to go with. On the more positive end we have a study from SmallBizTrends.com that showed the failure rate only at 71 percent,[49] and on the more nightmarish end, we have an article from Punch.com pointing out that out of one hundred businesses that start up today, only one will still be standing in ten years.[50] As a matter of fact, according to a Gallup poll, 45 percent of businesses with fewer than five employees (which is most businesses) have owners who have second jobs just to keep the business going.[51] This number actually increases when you account for the number of businesses that may have a spouse's income keeping them open.

Here is the real opportunity.

You, after reading this book and attending the workshops, know that the other twenty-five "mom-and-pops" statistically find themselves in the just-described nightmare. That means there are twenty-five offices, twenty-five secretaries, twenty-five accounting firms, twenty-five suppliers, twenty-five state license fees, and so on.

After making some calls, you get twenty of these companies to meet with you. Your plan is to create a new pest control company and merge as many of these mom-and-pops together as possible. You explain to these business owners that you understand their situation and how they are living a nightmare.

Ten of the twenty-five decide to join you. The other fifteen are stubborn and full of pride or maybe one or two are above water.

The new company is formed under the premise that you get 25 percent of the initial increase in profit and 10 percent from then on. The ten incoming owners split the new company in proportion to what they bring to the new company. For example, if Bob's company brings in 550 clients and that makes up 18 percent of the new company's client base, he starts with 18 percent ownership.

Ten companies paying ten secretary/managers $35,000 a year is $350,000. By merging the companies into a new company, you only need two office staff at a salary increase to $40,000 a year each. You just increased profits by $270,000. No new customers, and already there is a quarter of a million dollars in profit. Going from $5,000 per company paid to their respective accounting firms down to one accounting firm increases profit another $45,000. And so on and so forth.

The management structure of the new company results in seven out of the ten owners not wanting the headache of management, so they elect to be working owners, out in the field providing the quality and service only an owner can. The other three owners are placed in management positions as voted on by the group (CEO, COO, and Sales VP), and you are chairman of the group. As chairman, you lead weekly meetings and the group as a whole, and you use your skill set (with the agreement of the group) to work on expansion opportunities.

The ten owners are happy being free of their past nightmare, the company is large enough to compete locally for those larger accounts held in the past by the two national names in town, and you are the owner of the third-largest pest control company in your market, without even stepping on a spider. Not to mention, you pocketed more than $78,000 ($315,000 increase in profits just by consolidating staff and accounting firms × 25 percent = $78,750) right away on the profit created from the merger alone. Not bad for a few weeks of meetings and negotiations. The remaining fifteen pest control operators who didn't join the new company are one by one going out of business, and your new company is picking up some of their clients by default.

Profitable, or Profitable in Our Head?

I tell listeners of my radio show that everything works on paper. Politicians propose legislation because it works on paper. The president engages in what is supposed to be a six-month operation that turns into a fourteen-year war because the original plan worked on paper. Millions of "out of business" owners went into business because it worked on paper.

When looking at a business, you need to determine not if you will make a profit on paper, but if you could make a profit in the real world.

Let's use a restaurant as an example.

You decide you can make eggs and toast as well as your favorite greasy spoon. You look at the bulk price of eggs and bread only to discover that while you paid $7 for two eggs, toast, hash browns, and coffee, that whole meal only cost the restaurant $1.10 in inventory.

Because it worked on paper, you take out a second mortgage on the home and open your restaurant.

5,000 square feet of space at $15 per square foot plus common area maintenance (CAM) on a triple net lease = $8,000/month

Electric, gas, and water = $540/month

Phone and internet = $300/month

A small ad in the phone book = $400/month

You know as well as I do that there are more monthly expenses than that. Also, that $8,000 a month for rent came with a lease that lasts for ten years, for a total of $1.1 million. The existing space is not set up for a restaurant, so construction and kitchen renovations cost you $165,000, but you also have a second mortgage on a ten-year note at 5 percent, for another $1,958.41 per month expense ($235,005 over ten years). Let's estimate that total expenses are on the very low end of $1.335 million for ten years, meaning you need to bring in $11,125 a month just to pay the expenses at the restaurant. You know now what the practical poverty level is, which means that to cover your personal monthly expenses, you need an additional $6,000 a month in income.

This means that your total monthly expenses between business and personal life are $17,125. Keep in mind that in this example you have no employees yet, so with these numbers you are the owner, cook, waiter, janitor, menu designer, decorator, and bookkeeper. If your business is open six days a week, you are working twelve hours a day at least. Then on the seventh day, you need to catch up on the bookkeeping for a few hours. In this example you are broke, but making the bills. This is pretty likely to be the case, right?

At $7 per breakfast, giving you a $5.90 markup and $1.10 to pay for the food, you need 2,902 customers per month, or 670 per week, or 112 per day. If you are open from 9 A.M. to 9 P.M., that is more than one meal served every six and a half minutes of every day. If a meal isn't ordered every six and a half minutes, you are in the red! Red means going backward, meaning that even if you do serve one order every six and a half minutes (which is almost impossible as a one-person operation), you are still not profiting, you are just getting back to zero at the end of each month.

The "everything is profitable in our head" problem doesn't just apply to small businesses. According to the *Dallas Morning News*, from 2001 to 2010 the aviation industry only made a profit in three of those years; as a group, the industry lost more than $54 billion in that same period for a net loss. The article goes on to point out that from 1947 to 2010, the entire industry is still at a loss. It quoted Warren Buffett as saying: "The worst sort of business is one that grows rapidly, requires significant capital to engender the growth, and then earns little or no money. Think airlines. Here a durable competitive advantage has proven elusive ever since the days of the Wright Brothers. Indeed, if a farsighted capitalist had been present at Kitty Hawk, he would have done his successors a huge favor by shooting Orville down."[52]

You need to find opportunities in which if you only make 25 percent of your projected profits you will still achieve your objectives. Compare that to your restaurant example, in which even if you were to hit 100 percent of your payment obligations, it still doesn't make sense to pursue the opportunity.

Does It Fit Your Vertical Alignment, Goals, and Exit Plan?

If your vertical alignment includes the priority of spending quality time with a spouse, would our restaurant example fit as an opportunity that empowers you to work your vertical alignment? No, because you would be working twelve-hour days on the open days and several hours of back-end work on the closed day. Would the company formed by creating a merger in the pest control industry fit that vertical priority? Yes, because it required a few weeks of meetings and negotiations to get to profitability, and the newly formed management team eliminates heavy time requirements on your part.

If the goal is to raise $1 million in profit in order to move the family to South America and leave "the system" in the next five years, would a profitable business giving you plenty of family time and $70,000 a year in take-home profit fit that goal? No, because while profitable and aligned with your vertical alignment of family time, you cannot meet your ultimate objective. You would need a business that either generates $1 million in profits over the next five years, or has sales high enough to warrant a $1 million price tag if you sold the business.

If your exit plan (which will be explained in more detail in the next chapter) is to sell a company in five years and then retire to the Bahamas, would a franchise requiring a twenty-year contractual commitment be a fit for your plan? No. It doesn't mean the business is bad, nor does it mean that an opportunity doesn't exist; it just doesn't fit in your objective. This is why it is *so* important to have your vertical alignment, your *why*, and your exit plan in place before moving forward and opening your business.

When you select a business that doesn't facilitate your vertical alignment, goals, and exit plan, you no longer own the business—the business owns you, regardless of the business's ability to make a profit! This is such a common yet unrealized problem that people seek therapy to be happy in their profitable business careers. Even though they are making money, they are not feeling productive or fulfilled. There are even articles, books, and seminars based on helping people get the passion and spark back into their business life. Those business owners are not involved in a business that empowers them to work their vertical alignment, achieve their goals, and design their exit. The worst part of this problem is that most of those business owners and the "experts" they turn to do not even know this aspect of the process is missing! Fewer still place these elements of vertical alignment and goal achievement into the equation of determining whether a business is qualified for their opportunity basket before they started their business, let alone what an opportunity basket (the process of evaluation) is.

When you use these four factors to determine whether a business is right for you, you are among the elite in business and in life.

EVANGELPRENEUR ACTION STEP

Make a list of no less than twenty-five opportunities for your opportunity basket. No two opportunities should be similar. For example, a bakery, a deli, and a bagel store would not all be allowed, because they are too similar. Also, no more than half of the opportunities should be in an industry in which you have expertise and experience.

By the time you make your move as an Evangelpreneur, this list should double in size to fifty. Once you get in-depth training, you will find that you continually place new opportunities in your basket. Even a bad economy or poor political conditions will not cast a shadow on your daylight, because when you can identify opportunities at the drop of a hat, the fear of not having options and alternatives goes away. You will always have a backup plan for you and your family, and simultaneously find yourself in a position to live a life of fulfillment.

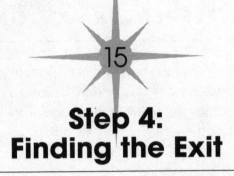

Step 4:
Finding the Exit

How to Get Out of Business Successfully

W HEN YOU BOARD AN AIRPLANE, the
flight crew points out the exits before the
plane lifts off. When you are in school, you
do fire drills to see how quickly everyone
can reach the exits. When I first enter a theater, restaurant, or any building, I always scope out the exits. The
Bible and the Christian faith (most faiths, actually) is all
about how you exit!

When you are determining how to pick a starter
business, enter the industry, and get started, you also
need to plan how you are going to exit. Even before you
settle on a certain business, you need to settle on how you
are going to leave it. If your goal is to leave the business
in five years and become a full-time missionary, you need

to determine the exit plan before you come up with your entry plan. If you plan on running the company until you are eighty-two and then handing it down to your children and grandchildren, you need to have an exit plan before you even open the doors.

In a sense, the exit plan lets us reverse-engineer the entire business plan. Reverse-engineering is how companies and nations discover unknown technology secrets, and it should be how business owners plan their future.

I have seen far too many business owners start a business, and then get stuck with it for decades because they didn't know how they were going to exit. I have seen business owners feel like they are no longer accomplishing what God has called them to accomplish, because they have locked themselves into a situation and don't see a way out.

Your Type of Business Affects Your Exit

Because the exit is so important to design before you even enter, you need to consider your desired exit when selecting the right business.

For example, if you are thinking about entering the tech industry with a company that will make phone apps, you need to have a short- and long-term exit plan with a heavier focus on the short term. When it comes to phone apps, there always seems to be a better one just months down the road. If you are stuck in multi-year leases and long-term agreements with your management team because you think you are going to be the next Google, you are not planning wisely.

That is not to say you are doomed to fail, nor does it suggest that you cannot morph your business as technology develops. You just need to realize that in your industry, a year in business is considered an amazing success.

So what would an exit plan look like in this scenario?

You find creative workspace, giving you freedom in terms of length of commitment. You assemble your management team and include specific clauses in their agreements. For example, you may write in, "If the company does not develop a new product offering every six months, then the duration of this agreement will conclude when sales of the last offering drop below $5,000 per month."

Another example would be a new energy company with an aftermarket product that allows cars to run on waste products like cooking oil or even water. Your up-front costs are heavy and require a lot of equipment, parts, and development. You start the business with just the desire to make a product and no real planning on how to get out, so the debt load in the initial startup can be quite extensive. A year into your company, you have a small manufacturing facility and a handful of working models. Your plan is to submit your product for approval in all fifty states, comply with automotive and pollution regulation, and then start selling. However, a major automotive manufacturer approaches you and offers to buy your company, or more specifically your patent, and start putting the product in their vehicles in the upcoming model year.

What do you do? Do you negotiate a royalty for every unit sold? Do you agree to allow them to use the technology in their vehicles, but reserve the right to continue developing and selling your product to vehicle and heavy equipment manufacturers outside of the automaker's scope of products? Are you obligated to pay your crew a percentage of any offers that are accepted? By having one or more exit plans, it empowers you to make smart decisions while also achieving your objectives.

Shark Tank: Have an Exit Plan

I recently was having a conversation with Kevin O'Leary (Mr. Wonderful of the hit ABC show *Shark Tank*), and we were discussing the prevalence of business owners not having an exit plan, which results in them suffering disaster, pride, and greed. He said that there are so many examples of business owners or inventors coming on the show who only have a plan to get money to grow their company and are completely unprepared for any curveball thrown their way. Kevin may offer a large amount of money for a large percentage, but because the business owners don't have an exit plan and don't know their *why* well enough, they turn down (often due to pride and greed) what most of us would think is a great offer. They usually get upset by the large percentage Kevin wants to take, in some cases in exchange for a royalty for the entrepreneurs, which could actually make them millionaires. Instead, they refuse the offer and their businesses don't grow. Even though the offer was high, they just didn't have in their planning the thought of selling off part or all of the company, typically because the business itself became the focus of activity rather than being just a means to an end, that end being their *why*.

Notice how all the areas we have been talking about tie into each other? Your *why* and your vertical alignment impact your exit plan. Your exit plan impacts your opportunity basket, and your ability to put the recipe together determines your success.

EVANGELPRENEUR ACTION STEP

Once you know your vertical alignment, your *why*, and how to identify business opportunities, start adding to the business assessment, and determine your ideal exit.

Identify not only the reason a quick or delayed exit time line may be appropriate, but integrate your *why* and vertical alignment into that equation.

When you do this, you will start to realize that because your vertical alignment and your *why* are more important to you than the business itself, you have many exit options. As a matter of fact, as an Evangelpreneur you should be looking for and willing to walk away from your business in a moment's notice if a different opportunity for you to pursue your *why* and vertical alignment is presented. Evangelpreneurs are a stark contrast from business owners who put their businesses first and hold on too tightly, for too long, and to the detriment of other areas of their lives.

Take a look at the businesses you have in your opportunity basket and determine about a half-dozen possible exit scenarios.

There is no way to predict every exit opportunity, but by identifying a number of potential exits for a number of potential businesses, it will train your mind to recognize an exit when it does present itself.

Step 5:
Putting the Recipe Together

Getting Started

AM NO CULINARY MASTER; that is for sure. My signature dish is any meat product that I can put on an open flame—and even then, often the food ends up in worse condition than the charcoal it was cooked over. Despite my limited cooking ability I was asked to be a celebrity guest on the cooking show *What's Cooking with Doc*, hosted by a trained chef, Dr. Michael Fenster, who also happens to be a licensed cardiac surgeon.

One of the things I learned from experiencing a crash course in cooking in front of a television audience was that the recipe is important. If you want to make a great dish, you have to know what ingredients you need before you turn on the stove. You cannot expect to make a cake if you don't first make sure you have eggs, butter, flour, and so on. Once you have the ingredients, you cannot just throw all the products in a bowl and expect to have a cake. There is an order, in which each ingredient is prepared or mixed with others, that is essential to transforming the group of ingredients into a cake. Adding the frosting right after you put the eggs in the bowl would result in an inedible mess.

A recipe is not just a list of ingredients. A recipe is a list of ingredients *and* instructions on how much of each ingredient you will need, as well as an outlined plan of implementation and preparation.

The same is true in business. If you want a successful dental practice, for example, then you need many ingredients and a recipe to put it all together. The ingredient list for an open and profitable dental practice would include some of these tasty ingredients of success:

- Sales skills
- SEO proficiency
- Advertising awareness
- Branding execution
- Supply chain participation
- Competitive analysis and planning
- Marketing ability
- Negotiation proficiency
- Mental processing understanding

- Laddering ability (a communication skill for eliminating disagreement)
- Social media proficiency
- Female and male variance awareness
- Profit partner development
- Effective networking
- Workplace efficiency
- Goal planning and achievement
- Leadership development
- Influence proficiency
- Support network acquisition
- Capital strategy
- Outside opportunity sourcing

And this is just for starters!

The problem is, using a dental practice as an example, most dentists go to dental school, maybe take one elective course about running their own practice, and then launch their business. After a few years, if the practice makes it that long, they start to wonder why they are not having the successful experience they wanted when they envisioned starting their own practice.

This is why you, as a current or future Evangelpreneur, cannot just take whatever you have now on your skill set shelf, throw it in a business, and expect it to work. It will just end up like the cake, a very expensive and emotionally draining mess.

If you really want to succeed in business, you need to invest time and money in learning how to acquire the needed ingredients for success, as well as how to use them. You will notice things like Small Business Administration (SBA) loans, business plans, and build-out blueprints are not listed. This is because those things and other related aspects of business are what I call "mechanical." I am not saying the mechanical parts are not important, but you can hire others to manage these parts of your business.

If your daughter was about to turn sixteen and start driving, would you, after fully explaining the workings of the internal combustion engine, then hand her the keys to your car and tell her she is ready for her first interstate road trip to Florida? Of course you wouldn't, because she would crash before she leaves the neighborhood.

Mechanical knowledge alone does not enable your daughter to know how to drive a car. If one day the check-engine light comes on, does she need to know as much as a mechanic? No, she just needs to know where to find one.

The Mechanics of Business Are Not Enough

In business, we have a tendency to focus on the mechanical side (profit-and-loss sheets, SBA loans, shipping prices, etc.). I believe this is because it gives us the excuse of saying we are trying and learning, but we know we really are not doing all that is necessary, and having an excuse for failure feels good. We don't want to get outside of our comfort zone in order to learn to drive our businesses, so instead, we blame bad mechanical efforts for our failure.

> We don't want to get outside of our comfort zone in order to learn to drive our businesses, so instead, we blame bad mechanical efforts for our failure.

Too many authors, speakers, and experts focus on the mechanics of business for the same reason. They focus on mechanical issues such as profit-and-loss sheets, SBA loan applications, and so on, because they don't really know how to teach business owners how to drive a business.

Unfortunately, there are many business owners who, when trying to do the right thing and seek out continual training, find ill-equipped trainers and experts who, once again, just pile on more mechanical instruction.

This mechanical approach is, sadly, the focus of most business school programs, along with the tendency to teach what has already been done. While there is wisdom to be found in studying the work of those who came before us, we still need to recognize what those previous success stories really teach. What they really teach is that success in business actually comes from doing what other businesses have *not* yet done. School, whether business school or elementary school, tends to be less about finding the wisdom in the story of those who have come before, and more about what can be replicated by the masses, because only replication can be graded. Over the past three years alone I have had a number of business school professors on the program discussing this very issue, along with many MBA graduates, including one mentioned in this book, Dr. Michael Fenster, who also agrees with this statement. As a matter of fact, I conducted a Small Business Boot Camp on November 16, 2014, where a professor of business and economics from the University of Wisconsin system was in attendance, and it was wonderful having him confirm this point right there in the class. If this is the case, then we should expect and are now experiencing a high failure rate in business.

The mechanical side of things should not be a business owner's focus; instead, the focus should be getting those driving elements, those ingredients to success I listed previously, into our recipe. When business owners and soon-to-be business owners realize that focusing on the mechanical is not enough, and they go looking for training elsewhere, they need to know how to identify a qualified teacher.

There are many "motivational" and "leadership" trainers in the marketplace, some of whom are very famous,
but their teaching is built on sand.

*"Therefore whosoever heareth these sayings of mine,
and doeth them, I will liken him unto a wise man, which
built his house upon a rock: And the rain descended, and
the floods came, and the winds blew, and beat upon that
house; and it fell not: for it was founded upon a rock. And
every one that heareth these sayings of mine, and doeth
them not, shall be likened unto a foolish man, which built
his house upon the sand: And the rain descended, and the
floods came, and the winds blew, and beat upon that house;
and it fell: and great was the fall of it."* —Matthew 7:24–27

The reason why so many speakers, experts, and trainers
hide behind the "motivational" or "leadership" moniker
is because it is easy to fluff up. All you have to do is put
together some motivational quotes, get the audience
laughing and artificially pumped up, and you are on
your way to becoming an "expert" in motivation and
leadership. There are actually online classes and videos
on how to become an "expert professional speaker" in
less than a weekend. This is why people who attend these
events are excited for a few days, but after that, when
the euphoria wears off, the audience starts to realize that
the only real benefit they gained from the event was a
few clichéd quotes they can post on Facebook. They were
not provided with the real tools or the real instruction

needed to drive their business and their life toward their goals.

This is not meant to be a criticism of all speakers and experts. A number of motivational and leadership speakers offer something of value. However, the vast majority are poor speakers and experts who are trying to get money even though they offer nothing of real value. Because I am urging you to invest time and money by seeking out proper training, I thought it was necessary to provide my perspective.

With that said, let's take a look at four of the ingredients of success that I listed.

Sales

Sales are vital to everyone. Routinely, I will ask my seminar attendees, "Who is in sales?" and usually a couple of hands go up. I ask this question at churches, business forums, community events, and so forth. The truth of the matter is that regardless of where I ask this question, every hand should go up.

It doesn't matter if you are a doctor, a stay-at-home mom, a pastor, or even my editor who edited this book—everyone is in sales!

That thought tends to make us a bit queasy, but why? The reason is because we all have a predetermined and negative image of sales and salespeople. The universally held negative image is of someone who will try to pressure you into something you don't want or push you to make a decision, or worst of all, persuade you to buy something you really have no interest in. So powerful is this image that customers will be leery of dealing with a businessperson out of fear that this image may come true. In addition, many businesspeople will not actually engage fully in the sales process because they don't want to be viewed as that negative image.

Sales isn't a negative thing; to the contrary, sales is a great and powerful thing that, when done right, we don't even realize a sale has happened. A marriage proposal is a sale, enlisting in the military is a sale, getting your kids to go to bed is a sale. It is only when money exchanges hands that we get a nasty feeling and image about sales.

The problem, however, is that we are all in sales. The doctor has to sell his pharmaceutical rep on giving him a discount, or sell a patient on why they should have surgery. The stay-at-home mom needs to sell her kids on why they need to work hard on their schoolwork, and sell the babysitter on why working an extra hour tonight is better than going to that party. Even the pastor needs to sell the idea of small groups or church expansion. As funny as it may sound, even editors and authors sell to each other. An editor needs to sell an author on the changes suggested to the book in a way to get it into the best possible condition to attract readers, and authors sell editors on why a new concept, while it may be counter to what is commonly accepted as standard, is the direction the teaching needs to go to best convey the book's new information and new way of thinking.

Since this is the case and we are all in sales, we need to really look at what "sales" is.

My definition of sales: *Facilitating an execution of an existing belief and/or the guidance to a new belief to the mutual benefit of the provider and recipient.*

To grasp the depth of this definition we could cover what a belief is, how it is created, and how it operates. Unfortunately, we have neither the time nor the space for that in this book.

However, what we can address here is the image. The reason we have such a bad image of sales is because "sales techniques" are used to manipulate us into doing something. Those who teach these techniques don't understand my definition, so there is a lot of manipulation involved in today's marketplace.

The reason we have such a bad image of sales is because "sales techniques" are used to manipulate us into doing something.

Consider this: Sundays are the busiest days for car lots in the state of Wisconsin. This is neither because people are not working on Sundays nor because people do all their errands on Sundays. The reason why Sundays are the busiest days is because the car lots are closed. You can drive by a car lot on Sunday in Wisconsin and see people looking at cars and trucks by the droves. Yet on Monday morning the sales team shows up and doodles on their business cards, because nobody has come by the dealership yet.

A car dealer in Madison, Wisconsin, explained to local station CBS Channel 2 the phenomenon about Sunday car "shopping." He said, "A lot of people, they want to go out and look, and they don't want to be bothered."[53] Car shoppers want to look without being pitched. We all can understand why: Nobody likes being sold.

Because we hate "sales," business owners (and everyone else for that matter) make a huge mistake—they tend to avoid sales training. This is disastrous, because every business relies on sales. When we open a business and think we don't need sales training, or we don't want to become a "salesman," we abandon one of the most important, if not *the* most important, parts of running a business.

Consider this: Coca-Cola spends billions on advertising. Coke is the world's most recognized brand. Coke has a huge sales force. You would think that the most recognized brand in the world and one of the largest companies on the planet wouldn't need salespeople. But, not only does the company have legions of salespeople, it spends a fortune on training them.

Because we hate "sales," business owners (and everyone else for that matter) make a huge mistake—they tend to avoid sales training.

You probably do not have a multibillion-dollar-a-year marketing budget. Odds are, you do not have the world's most recognized brand. Odds are, you are not investing in sales training.

As a warning, I will tell you that there are sales programs out there that teach you to sell with methods that do more harm than good. I can think of only five trainers I would send my friends to (of course, I'm one of them), so be very careful when you select your sales training, but please recognize that you need it.

Advertising Awareness

One of my favorite topics to cover is advertising; it's everywhere, yet even the people who sell it don't seem to understand it.

As business owners, we know we need to advertise, and we could spend a whole day talking about where, how, social media, billboards, and so on, but the bottom line is we know we need to do it.

Many startups either don't spend money and/or effort on advertising because they think they don't need to, or they spend money on the wrong media, which becomes a waste.

To make the problem worse, most people don't understand what successful advertising looks like. I can always identify a rookie when we discuss advertising; they want to talk about ROI (return on investment). They have the idea that if they spend a thousand dollars in advertising this month, they will expect to see an ROI of say, $10,000 this month.

That is *not* how advertising works. That sounds more like marketing, and there is a huge difference. Let's say a company spent a thousand dollars on an advertising campaign. The potential customer was exposed to the ad. The customer likes the product; let's say it's a new fishing pole. But, because he needs to wait until he gets his bonus check in two months, the purchase is delayed.

Was the advertising a failure? No. Unfortunately, many uneducated business owners would feel as if it was. The advertising they did this month exposed their brand and their product to someone who will be willing and able to purchase it in two months. The small business owner usually looks at the end-of-month results, and says that because they didn't sell more products, they are discontinuing their advertising. This has a fallout effect, because in two months, when the man who wanted their fishing pole is ready to buy it, he has forgotten who the company was due to the lack of consistent advertising. He instead buys the pole from the company that advertises all the time on the Sportsman Channel.

Again, this is just an example and there is so much more to learn, but it shows how getting advertising training is important.

Social Media Proficiency

Oh, social media; what a crazy technological development. Social media has a tendency to make us less social. Recently on my talk show I was covering how social media is affecting the next generation, specifically how social functions once held dear are falling out of favor. Here's an example looking at a school profiled in a *Business Insider* article: In 2001, 800 students attended the school dance. In 2010, that number was down to just 26. By 2014, the school dances were canceled. The school didn't shut down, and it didn't shrink in size. The reason why school dances no longer take place is because of social media. When the reporter asked one student the reason for this, she concluded that the students "would rather be home texting, Facebook messaging, or Snapchatting each other."[54] The reporter found this to be the case with other schools in the area as well. Today's kids don't have as much of an interest in truly being social when they can pretend to be social with a device in their hands.

This isn't a phenomena limited to youth. Parents in their thirties and forties are increasingly guilty of ignoring their children and their spouses, because they are so distracted by social media. I remember one guy who contacted my show and told a story about taking his wife out to dinner at a nice place, so they'd have a chance to get away from the house. They dress up a bit, make a dinner reservation, and he even puts in the effort to clean the minivan. At dinner, she spends the entire time updating social media, posting pictures of her food, and even runs to the bathroom to check an incoming post. When the idea of no phones at dinner or on date night is suggested, a fight follows. And it's not just date night. I have spoken with, and worked with event planners, wedding planners, and even funeral directors who have told me family reunions, weddings, and funerals are all seeing a decline in attendance due to the increased reliance on social media to stay connected.

The reality is that in many ways social media is like Pandora's box. From a business perspective, there is a knee-jerk reaction from small business owners to not only get their businesses involved in social media, but in many cases, rely on it for the majority of customer generation.

Since Facebook's initial public offering, many have complained about how ineffective it is for business generation. It turns out that people don't like to be pitched by companies while they are trying to be social. How ineffective is social marketing? An IBM report found that social media platforms combined accounted for 0.34 percent of all online sales generation. Not 34 percent, 0.34 percent, less than one-half of one percent. Out of all the platforms, Twitter fared the worst with zero effectiveness.[55]

There is some basic truth behind their stance. Let's say you have a small maple syrup business and you delve into social media. Let's also say you have 10,000 Facebook followers. The way Facebook's algorithm works, your post will only be posted on 6 to 19 percent of your followers' social media pages. This means your post will only appear on 600 to 1,900 people's pages. This is why social media companies want to sell your business a service that will place your post on more of your follower's pages. In 2012, PageLever conducted a study that found if you have 1,000 to 10,000 followers on Facebook, your post will appear on the Timeline of only 19 percent of them. (In 2021, it's even worse.) The same study also found that if you become more successful in getting followers, your percentage actually goes down to as low as 6 percent of your followers seeing your post if you have more than one million followers.[56] Another study conducted in February 2014 by Social Oglivy found the outlook even worse, with only 2.11 percent of followers seeing a post in their Timeline.[57] This point was driven home in 2019 when social media effectiveness was declining even further. A popular social media influencer with 2.6 *million* followers failed to sell thirty-six shirts. Not 36,000. Not 3,600. Not 360. Thirty-six shirts![58]

Now, let's say you post on a social site at 4 P.M. Not only will only 19 percent of your followers have it posted to their feed, but because the average user has hundreds of friends who also post, by the time these followers actually go on Facebook, they have posts from hundreds of other sources to scroll through to even see yours. By the time they check their feed, at 7 P.M. for example, they would have to scroll down too far to see your three-hour-old post, and they are unlikely to see it.

If half of the 600 to 1,900 who got your post see it, you have 300 to 800 pairs of eyeballs. Let's be optimistic and say that half of those people who actually had your post on their Timeline see it, this means you have a possible quality exposure rate of 150 to 400 people. While 150 exposures out of 10,000 people may excite you, it would be unlikely and unrealistic to count on a purchase from any of them. Yet, there are small business owners relying on this as their main source of business generation. Tomorrow, will you do the same process and hope for a different result?

Now, to make it even worse, this is not really quality marketing and it certainly isn't advertising. Advertising is an effort to make the most people possible aware of your brand through the media used. Just think about this for a second. You are posting on people's pages who are already aware of you. In a perfect world maybe a friend or two of theirs will see it, but now we are actually talking about a fraction of a fraction, such as only 150 out of 10,000 seeing your post. If 10 percent hit "like," which is actually a high percentage, that means fifteen people responded. Out of the fifteen who responded (that does not mean they purchased), maybe one of their friends will show on their Timeline that they liked your page, thus going back to the percentage stats on those who actually see the post about a friend liking a page, giving us maybe rapidly shrinking exposure rate once it gets past the first person who responded. At best, you are improving customer retention.

Since it is not advertising, it does fall, by loose definition, into the category of marketing; it does represent a focused effort to create a course of action among a predetermined demographic of previous customers and those exposed to the brand in the past. Even then, though, social media marketing is little more than a necessary evil. There are exceptions to the rule. For example, Poo-Pourri, which is a liquid you spray in the toilet before you use it, has had huge success using social media, which makes sense because the medium fits the product and its branding perfectly. Sadly, however, many of the tens of millions of businesses in the United States approach social media as their number-one effort to drive sales, and they are failing.

PCWorld magazine ran an article about how social media is not as effective as business owners think it is, or need it to be. As part of the article the reporter looked at a business that had 145,000 likes on its Facebook page; when the company spent $60,000 on social media advertising, it had "almost no effect."[59] Yet there are "experts" out there talking about how social media needs to be your focus and how you should spend your money on this medium.

Does this mean you shouldn't be involved in social media? No, there is a role for it, but you should approach it in the proper way. When using social media you need to keep a few things in mind:

1. Your posts should only promote you and your business 10 percent of the time at the max. Anything more and people will feel like all you are doing is trying to drum up business.
2. Your social media needs to match your branding. The companies that have the worst social media response are those that are branded in a corporate

way (think IBM or Coke), while the more successful ones are branded around a personality (think Flo from Progressive Insurance).

3. Lower-cost products or services have higher response rates. Knowing that those who follow you already know about you, ask yourself how likely it is that your customers are going to buy based on your posting. If you are a hair stylist, your response rate will be much higher than a Realtor's, whose customers only shop every so many years.

4. Calculate the cost. Because social media is so addictive, you can easily spend hours on the internet thinking you will drive up sales. But if you notice the response is not there or sales are not increasing, your time would be better invested elsewhere.

5. Realize the benefit might be different than what you think. For example, having 100,000 followers who rarely respond is useless for driving business. However, using your follower numbers in other marketing efforts can have a benefit—for example, putting the fact that you have 100,000 followers on Facebook in your printed material conveys that you must know what you are doing and your product/service must be good.

Even after you are trained on how to properly approach social media, you should never count on it as your main source of new business.

Leadership Development

Poor approach to leadership is one of my pet peeves. Not only is this area of business dominated by fairly useless training, but even the limited amount of quality training we do find doesn't really apply to small businesses.

A common approach to leadership that leadership speakers embrace consists of addressing the topic as if those they are trying to lead actually *want* to be led. This is a completely false premise, and because of it, we see productivity and commitment declining in almost every sector.

When a professional sports coach writes a leadership book, his approach is leading people who all want to be led to the same goal. When an NFL player wants to make $16 million a year, he wants to be the best athlete on the field, and he wants his team to win the Super Bowl. It shouldn't be hard to persuade him to follow a leader that will allow him to make $16 million a year, become the best athlete on the field, and win the Super Bowl. I am not saying that the coach does not have great skills, but leading men who have spent countless hours playing for free, training for free, and who are now working in their dream career certainly requires a different form of leadership than leading a workforce that statistics show is not happy to be there, whose desires are not being met with the wages they receive. That is not to say employees are not hard working or lack expertise, but it is certainly a different form of leadership.

As a small business owner, the people you are leading usually do not want to be there. Here is a quick test: Are your employees happier on Monday morning or Friday afternoon? Exactly! Contrast that with the athlete who dreams of getting the chance to go to his place of work.

Some people call the current form of leadership "peak to peak," meaning it is from victory to victory, or happy place to happy place. It sees only the high points (peaks) in life, and is an approach to leadership that seems to believe nothing is ever wrong, so we just need to go from perfect to more perfect. Unfortunately, that is what I see in most leadership books and training. It is the easy leadership—the cheesy, clichéd form of leadership.

Talking about teams is fun, and team-building ropes courses are cool the first time, but how do you lead an employee who is going through a divorce? How do you get someone who sees layoffs to the left and right to be enthusiastic about becoming a key member of your inner team? If most leadership training weren't so sad, it would be funny.

Your employees don't want to work for you...Don't believe me? Stop paying them and see how many still show up.

As a real leader, as someone who is mixing your faith with your professional efforts, you are instead called to be a "valley-to-valley" leader. Such a leader doesn't pretend that everything is perfect, everyone is happy, and everything just works because we want it to. He or she is a leader that gets down in the dirt, in the pain, leading people through the valleys of life.

Let's just be honest for a minute. Your employees don't want to work for you. I don't care whose book told you otherwise. Don't believe me? Stop paying them and see how many still show up. Sure, we could say that if we don't pay sports figures their millions they would stop playing, but that really isn't the case. They played for free from when they were little kids to grown men; they just happen to have the extra element of being paid for it now. If you look back at the early days of the NFL, players actually lost money because they were players. Most needed off-season jobs just to pay the bills in order to play—very different from most professions. I cannot remember the last time someone came up to me and said, "Josh, I want to create an amateur league of receptionists. We want to get together every day just to randomly answer phones and type memos." Yet I do see dozens of leagues around my state alone for adults who want to play amateur football, baseball, soccer, and so forth. Does it matter that you made them feel special and shared a vision with them? Of course not.

To become real and effective leaders, we need to put all the "share a vision" and peak-to-peak leadership stuff on the back burner. We need to learn how to communicate and act in such a way that enables us to nourish the dreams of those being led, heal their pains, and bring them to a point where leadership transforms.

If a business is going to thrive, if achievement is going to be realized, and if Evangelpreneurs are going to have an impact, there needs to be a shift toward real leadership training.

We have just exposed and examined only four areas where you need to constantly train and grow. Each would require its own book if I were to teach all of the solutions to the listed issues, but my point was rather to drive home the message that you need to get real training. You need to admit that you do not have everything needed on your ingredient list, and that you don't know the recipe or the proper way to use each ingredient.

Growing in Wisdom

I remember talking to a guy on a plane. He was telling me what he did and that he had just talked to a consultant. He laughed and said, "I told that guy I don't like consultants, and I actually know how to run my business." This, of course, is one of the most ignorant comments I've ever heard.

Just think about this for a second. Even Google hires outside consultants and trainers on a regular basis. Google, which essentially invented its marketplace, uses consultants. (Yes, there were search engines before Google, but Google redefined the purpose of what a search engine does and certainly how it markets its services—through paying for ranking, ad-based results, marketing services, etc.—to become the giant it is today.)

Ronnie Coleman, eight-time "Mr. Olympia," has a trainer. You would think that the world's top bodybuilder would know how to build his body, but experts know they need to constantly seek out experts. Pilots, doctors, teachers, actors, writers, singers, and people in pretty much every profession that requires talent also need ongoing training—and they recognize that. How foolish and sad it is to see business owners full of pride say they don't need training. How egotistical and prideful it is to believe as a business owner that you have achieved expertise in all these areas of business operation in which you have never even engaged. Fear not, I too have made this mistake and had to learn from it. Even today I find myself seeking wisdom, training, and counsel in areas that I am not an expert. We wouldn't let our children act this way. If you had a daughter who played soccer and she was named the best player in the state, would you allow her to tell you she doesn't need to practice? Would you allow her to tell you she doesn't need to listen to the coach? The same principle applies to adults. Tiger Woods has a swing coach, for goodness' sake.

As a business expert and someone who believes in investing in small businesses, I can tell you that I would not invest in the company of someone who came to me and said, "Josh, I am an expert landscaping contractor. I have had the most profitable business in the industry statewide for three years now. I don't need to go to seminars. I don't need to read books on the issues you listed." Not only would I not invest in his company, I would probably laugh right in his face. People like that are called "future failures," and more often than not, they are failing in other areas of life as well, such as their health and relationships. Unfortunately they don't even realize how those private failures have a negative effect on their professional efforts as well.

As an Evangelpreneur, you need to make a constant and ongoing effort to invest time and money into perfecting all of those areas of business that are vital to driving your life to your goals. There are times where the ignorant suggest that there is no way people can master all of those areas, and that it would be better to just focus on the skill they use to perform the job itself—a plumber on plumbing or a furniture maker on making furniture, for example. Usually, this belief is illustrated with the expression, "Don't be a jack of all trades and a master of none." This has to be one of the most misused expressions. I want to ask these people: If they are a plumber, do they not know how to brush their teeth? Do they not know how to tie their shoes or drive a car? Do they not know how to swim or ride a bike? Why would they spend time learning hundreds of skills when they believe they should only be focusing on plumbing?

The reality is you can and need to learn hundreds of skills in life. Your business is a part of your life, and your business requires that you know how to be proficient in many skills. Becoming proficient in many skills does not diminish your area of expertise, just like knowing how to cook your own breakfast doesn't take away from your ability to dial a phone.

EVANGELPRENEUR ACTION STEP

Plan your first seminar attendance. Obviously, I would suggest attending one or more of mine, but even if it is not my training, you need to make the effort to get the education you need to make the recipe work. Do your research, and by that I mean stay away from the fluff- and motivation-centered events. Look for events where you will be entertained to remain engaged, but also learn real tools you can take with you afterward and use.

Take out your calendar and block out time *at least* once or twice a year to attend full-day or multi-day seminars. Do not think this is a one-time thing; training should be an ongoing learning opportunity for you until the day you die.

This leads us to budget. Do not skimp! Without training, your odds of failure skyrocket. If you think a seminar is expensive, consider the cost of failure. When a business opens, the business owner will spend hundreds of dollars on business cards, and thousands on signage, computers, point-of-sale systems, equipment, security, build-out, and more. Training is more valuable and more important to your success than any of those assets. If you don't know how to drive your business, the $2,000 computer system isn't going to do it for you. If you *do* know how to drive your business, you can make unlimited profits, even if you don't buy the $2,000 computer system. It is time we realize that training needs to be a major part of our lives.

Get your budget and calendar set for training!

PART 4

Doing Life

The Second Generation

Raising Your Kids to be Evangelpreneurs

B Y THIS POINT, you know the problems we are facing, the solutions, and even how to begin implementing those solutions (by being an Evangelpreneur!). But it doesn't stop with you. You want to pass on your new way of life to the next generation, and hopefully the ones that follow. You want to leave a legacy. And that's what this chapter is all about.

When the Scriptures tell us that we are to provide for our children and our children's children, the Bible is usually referring to financial provision. However, we cannot think we are supposed to simply leave behind a pile of money and hope for the best. Would a farmer store up his seed in an empty field and just hope that the pile survives rot, looting, and consumption by wild animals? Of course not. The farmer stores his seed in a location that is sheltered, secure from pillage, and in an environment that will prevent rot. This same care has to be given to what we leave behind.

Everyone is familiar with stories where kids inherit Mom and Dad's money, and the situation results in family rifts, overindulgence, and waste. This is not what God desires, I am sure. Also, the waste and family destruction would not allow the third generation to benefit.

As Evangelpreneurs, you may or may not be leaving behind a significant amount of money. A pile of money is nice if it is an extra benefit, but ultimately, your goal should be to leave behind a system or business that continues to provide income after your life on earth ends.

This does not mean that if you leave behind a business instead of or in addition to a pile of money, that greed and poverty won't happen. I have seen many families and businesses destroyed by inherited businesses. As a matter of fact, according to the Family Business Institute, only 30 percent of privately held companies will survive the second generation, 12 percent will make through the third, and only 3 percent will make it to the fourth generation and beyond.[60]

Sometimes it's not due to business failure but due to other factors. When I was working on the book *Quit Your Job or Die: Discover the Importance of Self-Employment*, I interviewed a very wealthy man who started a business that became successful. At the end of the interview, he voiced his concerns about the second generation coming after him. He had a couple of kids in their late teens, and neither expressed interest in inheriting the business that carried their name. His fear was that after he passed they would sell the business for a huge sum of money, which would "spoil" them to the point where they wouldn't strive for anything, work to better themselves, or stay close as a family.

Whether we leave behind a pile of money, a business, or a combination of both, we need to think about preparing the second generation to pick up where we leave off. There is a lot of consider. Should we expect them to have a passion for the business, even if they have different interests than we do? If they are going to pursue other careers, how do we prepare them to receive any prosperity we leave them and yet also buck the trend of children destroying themselves and the family with the inheritance?

Most of us want to work hard to bless future generations and give our kids the ability to prosper from our efforts. This is a good thing, but we need to address the fears and questions that we and the next generation have about how best to make that transition or pass down the assets or business. Some financially successful people, in an effort to prevent money from spoiling heirs or ripping a family apart, decide to leave the wealth and assets to charity as a way to make their kids earn their own way in the world. The theory goes that if the kids have to start from zero and work their way up, they may not have wealth, but they will grow to be well-rounded people. Sometimes that is the case. I say "sometimes" because in other cases, we see families get bitter when a loved one gives their money to charity when they pass. Often, this leaves the deceased's children feeling excluded from their parents' lives and legacies. Sure, sometimes that feeling comes from greed, but it also comes from feelings of being distrusted, unloved, unworthy, and unimportant.

As Evangelpreneurs, we need to develop a strategy that enables others to continue carrying our efforts.

Leading Our Children in Our Footsteps

The first question we need to address is, how do we prepare the second generation to pick up where we leave off? Preparing them can be a challenge, as your children have free will, and they are on their own walk. You cannot force them to do anything they are not willing to do.

Baby Steps: Teaching the Paul Principle

When Paul was making tallits (which, contrary to popular belief, were not tents but rather what would be more recognized as prayer shawls, or prayer closets) to fund his ministry, he wasn't doing so because he loved the work and dreamed of one day opening his own tallit shop. No, it was just a way for him to fund his real passion, which was spreading the teachings of Yeshua. When your kids are young, they often have something they are passionate about, or want to do or purchase. Use that as a bridge to teach them the Paul principle, that efforts to earn money are just a tool to reach a much larger goal. Work with them to do multiple activities that help achieve their goal. This can start young, at three or four years of age! Let's say they want to go to the circus, and it requires five "good kid stickers" on their reward board (this is currency for toddlers). Work with them on five different activities, which earn them stickers. While you are working with them, talk about how the important focus is the circus, and help them look for sticker opportunities all over the place, because how we get those stickers doesn't really matter much compared to the goal.

Making Strides: Instilling Entrepreneurial Principles and Habits

As your children get older, you can start developing more entrepreneurial principles. For example, if little Sally has a toy little Jenny wants, work with the two of them and teach them to negotiate a trade. Tell them along the way that the best trades are the ones in which both parties are happy with the exchange.

Next, introduce real, profitable entrepreneurship. If Billy is twelve years old, and wants a new telescope, instead of having a "chores and allowance" employment structure, help Billy develop three ways to use entrepreneurship to earn the funds. Here are a few possible examples:

1. Sell some of his assets (toys, baseball cards, clothes, etc.) at a garage sale; he sets the prices and works his own cash box.
2. Negotiate with him to determine a price you will pay him to wash the car.
3. Set a rate for his landscaping services and pitch it to the old lady next door who has a flower garden.

However you help Billy earn the money, the important parts of this exercise are making sure that your child is responsible for setting the price, doing more than one part of any income-generating activity, and has multiple activities—not just one chore or business. Let me explain each of these.

Setting the price.

Chores for allowance teaches your kid to work a job. In a typical workplace scenario, the boss defines the job duties and sets the wage, and the worker does the job and gets the wage. This is a terrible lesson for kids! By negotiating the duties and wage themselves, children learn to value themselves and their abilities more than if they were simply earning a set wage. They also learn the lesson of supply and demand: overcharge and they lose the bid, undercharge and it takes too long to achieve their financial goal.

Doing more than just one action.

If your child didn't have to take his or her own inventory of skills and assets, decide what he or she was willing to sell, set the price, deal with the customers, mind the till, and do the logistics (such as the setup and cleanup in the garage sale example), he or she would only see employment and not the other important parts of becoming an entrepreneur. By doing it the described way, with all of the auxiliary but vital tasks, not only is your child getting real entrepreneurial skills, but he also builds values and appreciation for himself and business ownership.

Multiple income activities.

By generating income from more than one activity, your child learns about looking for opportunities and entry points. This is one of the first steps of becoming an Evangelpreneur (after determining vertical alignment and the *why*), and it also helps children develop the ability to spot those opportunities and act upon them. By developing these skills, children will become well-rounded and prepared individuals for the rest of their lives.

Passing on Your Purpose for the Business

The next question is, should we expect our children and grandchildren to want to carry on the torch of our businesses? It is no longer a world where you might say, "My dad was a blacksmith, my grandfather was a blacksmith, so I am going to be a blacksmith." People now have endless options. However, it is not really the endless options that prevents most second and third generations from continuing their parents' legacy. The real problems are the following:

1. We don't define the purpose of our legacy and share that with our children;
2. The children hate what the business has done to the family; and
3. The children were not brought into the process of the business throughout their lives, and therefore don't feel the same commitment and investment to it that the parent does.

When you look at dynasty families like the Rothschilds, the Kennedys, or Vanderbilts, you notice that the family business doesn't matter. It is the family purpose that drives the family, not the actual business. The evidence is that the family business changes often: for instance, publishing, mining, and shipping. The business is not the goal, but the business funds the family goal, which in the Rothschilds' case was to acquire enormous political control over national governments around the world. If you are going to do your best to empower and encourage future generations to actually follow your lead, then you need to do more than get your vertical alignment and *why* in order. You have to bring your children on board with it and develop a family purpose.

Too often, we see parents who are so engrossed in their life's work that they ignore their family. Preacher's kids, for example, tend to rebel against the family and the faith. This is not because of the religion itself, but because the "religion" took Mom and Dad away, and left the kids with babysitters and video games. The next generation therefore has too much pain and associates the pain with the parents' religion. Conversely, there are missionary kids who have followed in their parents' footsteps for generations, because the parents involved the kids in the mission work. The kids understood what the family was doing and why it was so important, and they were able to work alongside their parents. When they are grown, they desire to continue to pursue what was important to them growing up—missionary work.

We see business working the same way. When you look at many American, Canadian, and European business owners these days, they allow the business to consume their time and fill the void that a healthy family should occupy. In the past, people from those regions worked their family into the business, the way we see many immigrants doing today. When that family comes over from Egypt or Thailand, they already know that business ownership is the only way to make life work. They start a restaurant, flower store, or medical practice, and the kids are in the back room playing. When the kids get older, they start helping out and are raised to take over the business. That's why we have fifth-generation Greek restaurants and fourth-generation herbal stores. The reason we don't see this in America any longer is because Americans are not raised to think in terms of entrepreneurship leading to freedom for our families as our immigrant counterparts do; rather, we view entrepreneurship as something to try if you have a cool idea, want to be rich, or something you avoid because it is too risky. When you *need* to succeed in entrepreneurship and you *see* that it is really the only key to providing for everyone in your family in order to create a new life from scratch, your business becomes your lifeline and your family bond. Our immigrant counterparts have *why*s that are life and death; Americans have *why*s like a bigger TV or good pensions.

As Evangelpreneurs, we need to get our family on board and involved in the pursuit of the *why*s.

If you do intend to hand down your business to the next generation, plan that transition before you leave this earth. Train the children in the business and tell them how the transition will work. Get them involved in how the distribution of ownership will happen if you have more than one child. While everyone may get an equal percentage of the revenue, who is going to be responsible for which parts of the business? Is it possible to split your particular business into divisions? Do you have a child who knows already they would rather be a nurse or truck driver? If so, what role will that child play in the transition? Maybe she will get a certain percentage of ownership in the form of a silent position, or perhaps a royalty that is understandably less than that of the kids who elect to carry on the business.

There are thousands of ways to plan the transition, but most parents don't plan it, and even fewer involve the kids in the plan, which causes problems with implementation.

If you follow the principles in this chapter regarding raising children to embrace entrepreneurship, sharing your business and its purpose with your children, and offering generational options to them, you will increase the likelihood of multiple generations carrying on the family purpose as well as the family business if it continues to be the best-suited funding vehicle for your needs. However, even if a child or two leave the family business, you have also equipped and trained them in matters of business that will help them in whatever career they choose.

Implementing and raising your children with Evangel-preneurship practices is a win-win.

EVANGELPRENEUR ACTION STEP

Even now, as Evangelpreneurship may be a new concept for you and your family, start getting the second generation involved in the process. If you do not have a business yet, start sharing with your children the fact that you are looking at starting one. Tell them why. If you already have a business, but you haven't been running the business and your life as an Evangelpreneur, explain to them the changes that are coming.

At this point, you already have your vertical alignment, you have your *why*, and you know you should be getting the second generation involved with those as well. Expand on that a bit and explain to them how business ownership done in the manner of an Evangelpreneur will help you, your spouse, and the family as a whole live out what has been taught so far in this book.

Explain to your children that you want them to get involved. Ask them how they initially envision that playing out. They do not have the final say, of course, but everyone will get on board and be excited about moving forward.

Retiring Evangelpreneur Style

A New Look at an Aging Problem

A S YOU HAVE LEARNED BY NOW, earning money in the same way as most of the world (via employment) is not the way we, as believers, should want for ourselves, nor what we should want to teach future generations. Yes, there are always going to be employees. No, it doesn't mean you are sinning if you are an employee, and yes, it is okay if you never become an Evangelpreneur. Owning a business doesn't save your soul, and employment doesn't condemn your soul in and of itself. Keeping in mind what we have already learned, we need to go beyond using our time to advance as Evangelpreneurs, and address the issue of retirement as well.

First, retirement as we know it in the Western world is a fairly new idea. Work until you are sixty-five, transform into a snowbird that flies to Arizona for the winter, golf on the weekends, and take RV trips a couple of times a year. This way of looking at aging has not always been the common perspective.

We also know by this point that, just as the middle class will not survive more than three generations, modern retirement is not surviving past the third generation, either. By this I mean the employment of the older generations is not enough to keep the family in the middle class—and allow for a comfy retirement—into the third generation, due to rising prices and inflation. This is why the normal worldly retirement is not going to work for most people under the age of sixty at the time of this publication.

Social Security is not sustainable; the Rule of 72 and your 401(k) doesn't keep up with inflation. Even if you do manage to save enough each month to make modern retirement viable, the governments of the world spend so much that increasingly more money is required to keep those beasts fed through rising taxes. As a CNSNews.com article pointed out, the U.S. federal government brought in a record $3.02 trillion in tax revenue,[61] yet still we are experiencing increases in debt and deficit as spending outpaces income. When the government is spending more than it takes in, counting on the government for retirement is not a smart idea. By now in this book you know that counting on employment for a solid pension really isn't a valid retirement plan, either, yet reliance on government and employment retirement plans are being taught out there in the world.

What, then, is retirement from a Biblical viewpoint supposed to look like?

When we talk about retirement, part of the problem with the conversation is that people are so afraid of the future that they almost shut down. We have a tendency to put our heads in the sand and pretend "the system" will somehow miraculously recover. Please understand that this mind-set may be the hurdle keeping you from finding real security.

Security—what an important word. When we talk about retirement and security, we really are talking about money and the ability to cover our future medical needs, housing, and food.

What the Bible Says about Retirement

Interestingly, when you look for Bible verses concerning retirement, you don't find anything. When referencing retirement, some Biblical scholars list verses like Luke 1:23: "And it came to pass, that, as soon as the days of his ministration were accomplished, he departed to his own house." This, of course, is not really talking about retirement; it is just providing us a time line of what was happening in the time line of Zacharias and his service in the Temple, which had a predetermined time and duration (a tool that Scripture uses to show us the exact day that Yeshua was born). In the modern world, believers want to make the Bible fit life as opposed to make life fit the Bible, so they pretend this is talking about retirement.

If retirement is part of life, and the Bible is supposed to be our guide through all of life, then why doesn't the Bible address retirement?

The answer is simple: You are not really supposed to retire.

In the Western world, we view retirement as this point in life when we get to stop doing the thing that takes up the majority of our time. For most of us, the majority of our time is spent working forty hours a week for forty years to earn money. Biblically speaking, that is not supposed to be the main thing in your life. The Bible tells us we are to serve and obey Elohim and spread the Gospel throughout the world as we make disciples. That is the main thing we are supposed to be doing with our lives. Does God want us to stop doing that when we turn sixty-five, and instead spend our time fishing? Of course not. The reason the Bible doesn't mention retirement is because as long as there is breath in your lungs and you are able, you are to be a living testimony.

The Bible views money in the way we defined it earlier: a tool that allows us to accomplish or purchase. The Scriptures tell us how to handle money as a tool, whether we are talking about sending a missionary into the mission field, providing for widows, giving to a ministry, or even paying employees.

The fact that we focus on retirement as the main aspect of getting older shows us how our focus has really been on money. This focus leaves many believers without instruction from the Word, because the Word doesn't instruct us to have or focus on a modern worldly version of retirement. The Bible talks about money so much that in the New Testament alone, Jesus talks more about money and possessions than He does about Heaven and Hell. Yet pastors don't instruct how to make, handle, or age with money, so believers often don't know how to handle aging and finance.

"But Josh, if I retire from the factory and I figure out how to get a good pension, wouldn't that allow me to spread the Word more in retirement and maybe even go on some missionary trips?" That is putting way too much control in everyone else's hands, instead of placing control in the hands of yourself and your God. A CNNMoney article pointed out that after the crash of 2008, residential wealth (that's our money) fell by $16.4 trillion![62] Hundreds of thousands of people lost part or all of their pensions, mutual funds, and 401(k)s, and as of late 2019, the economy still hadn't made an effective recovery. Then, of course, we got hit with the global COVID crisis. While the recession (defined as two consecutive quarters of falling gross domestic product) has been declared by the political system to have ended, recovery is far off. So terrible is the current economy that many of the areas that suffer from a recession are in just as bad of a situation as they were when the recession was technically still in effect. To make this worse, as of early 2021 China and Europe are in recession, the majority of CEOs in America fear the recession will come here due to COVID and President Joe Biden, and *The New York Times* is pointing out that the recession may last an exceptionally long time.[63] A recession without full recovery from a previous recession is a "double-dip," which could make the recession of 2008 look like a walk in the park.

Back to the recession, though: If you were planning on retiring during that time frame, and by no control of your own, lost half of your nest egg, how secure would you have been? The idea that markets have great average gains over the long term—which is what brokers will tell you that you shouldn't worry about in five, ten, or even fifteen years because it is the twenty-year average that matters—doesn't hold practical water, either. You cannot delay your retirement and the need for that money for twenty years, or even five. Can you imagine if the twenty-year delay excuse would work with your electric company? "Sorry, I cannot pay my bills this year. But over a twenty-year average I will be okay—so can I pay you in 2034?" Even if you go the route of market-based retirement planning alone, you miss the opportunity for real security as you age.

Retirement Bible Style: Save the Gravy

Security should look like this: scaling back your physical workload (i.e., the number of hours and type of work) as you age, while maintaining income and the ability to continue God's work. Let's also throw in the ability to pay for health care and provide for future generations.

That sounds like what you were going to get with the 401(k), right? Wrong. Notice how I stated "maintain income."

I call this "saving the gravy." When Thanksgiving would come around at my house, there was always more gravy made than what we actually needed. I am a fan of gravy, and because it was already made, I would ask that we save the gravy. You can use it the next morning with breakfast or with the leftover turkey, which always seemed to be more than we needed as well.

When I started applying this term to retirement, it seemed to fit, because while a 401(k) or getting a job as a greeter for a big-box store is common in retirement, these certainly aren't things you would want because they're so enjoyable. Your gravy, in terms of money and retirement, is your ability to use something you already have in a way that makes the future a bit more enjoyable. Let's look at two ways we can "save the gravy" as Evangelpreneurs, and have empowerment as we age.

Your gravy, in terms of money and retirement, is your ability to use something you already have in a way that makes the future a bit more enjoyable.

Our first example is that of an existing business owner. Pretend for a moment that you are a silversmith in the late 1700s. Your arms and back only have a few more years in them for this sort of work. Your business has been a true Evangelpreneur example and a marketplace ministry. You engrave a Jesus fish on the bottom of each product, you use profits to provide for widows and orphans, and your storefront serves as a Wednesday night Bible study location. Plus, when an evangelist came to town for a three-day revival, you closed up shop and posted a sign in your window to tell others where you were those days, because you had the freedom to do so.

Now, you know you cannot keep your business going forever, and those U.S. Revolutionary bonds you purchased are not going to cut it.

You decide to "save the gravy." On Monday morning, you place an advertisement looking for an apprentice. You enter an agreement with your new apprentice to train him in your trade, and in exchange, he will one day take over the business while paying you 25 percent royalties until your death. If you had children, the agreement could involve an additional smaller royalty for them that continues after your death for five years, for example. This would allow them the opportunity to use those funds to engage in their own Evangelpreneur pursuits. Better yet, one or more of them could become your apprentices (see chapter seventeen, "The Second Generation"). But for simplicity's sake, let's pretend you brought in an outside apprentice.

The apprentice loves the idea, because he gets world-class training along with his own business in the future, but is also actively engaged in building it now. You train him as well as you can, because his future success impacts your future income.

You like this agreement because it continues your legacy and income, and even allows you to live out your faith in a way that may lead the apprentice to your faith—or, if he is already a believer, to mentor him in the ways of an Evangelpreneur. Of course, the benefit of being able to grow the business upon your existing brand and customer base is also a major advantage to both of you as the transition takes place. You may be thinking that there is little control or high risk with this model, as the apprentice could run the business into the ground. But that problem is self-solving because during the years of mentoring him, if you see that he isn't running the business well, you can let him go and choose another apprentice. The fact is that by the time you step back, your apprentice has been successfully running the business in your stead for a year or two and has shown that he is just as competent as you.

That is a secure retirement! I would take this situation over a government pension any day of the week. You have control, you involve God in your professional life, and you live out your beliefs in a way that enhances the future. We can make it even better, though!

Let's continue pretending you are a silversmith and Evangelpreneur in the 1700s (a time traveler gave you this book, I guess), and you understand the importance of exit planning as well as the principles of filling your opportunity basket. Over the next five years, while you are training your apprentice and securing that bright future, you take some of your profits and save more gravy. Instead of buying that 1 percent interest-bearing American Revolutionary bond, you take $5 and invest it in a newspaper startup in town. Next month, you take $10 and invest it into a company looking to add more ships to its fleet of merchant craft. Over the next five years, you take your gravy (profit) and invest in thirty more companies. You may be thinking, "Five years is sixty months, shouldn't it be sixty companies?" No, you still need to enjoy life along the way.

When you retire, your silversmith shop is more profitable than ever, you are getting 25 percent off the top, and you are part owner of thirty other companies. Will all thirty succeed? No, as a matter of fact, twenty of them may be belly up. But, because you know how to pick quality opportunities, ten of them are bringing in money each month. Remember, if you had bought the bond on a $100 investment at 1 percent interest, it would get you $1 a year. If ten of your business investments provided a return of even $10 a month, you are making $1,200 a year. In the late 1700s, you would be the richest man in the neighborhood. Don't forget, you still get 25 percent of that silversmith money, too.

You now have time available to spend your mornings walking along the riverfront with your wife in conversation and prayer. Your days are divided among recreation, building relationships, and of course advancing the Kingdom of God. Your evenings are full of great food and laughter with family and friends. Once in a while, you even spend the day back at your old shop helping out and continuing to mentor your former apprentice.

If you study this book, and put your recipe together, you will be able to take advantage of great opportunities even in bad economic times. When the markets lose more than $16.4 trillion of people's personal money, you could be finding great wealth by finding expanding opportunities. We can see the window for opportunity in the wake of the 2008 recession. In March of 2014, *Time* published a story that revealed that right before the stock market crash, there were 6.7 million US households with a net worth of more than a million dollars. The same magazine article revealed that even though most people were feeling the economic crunch, the number of households with a net worth of more than a million jumped to 9.2 million.[64] In bad economic times, the US added 2.5 million millionaires! By 2019, we were up to 11.8 million millionaire households, and this upward trend showed no signs of slowing coming out of the pandemic in Spring 2021.[65] The reason that the number of wealthy households grew is because those who were able to identify opportunities grew their net worth, regardless of the economic situation.

While we used an example of a silversmith from the 1700s, there is nothing stopping Evangelpreneurs from doing the same thing today. When we look back to 1700s America, when most people were business owners, the outlined retirement plan fits like a hand in a glove. However, when we look at the same plan and apply it to today's world, a world largely void of free-enterprise education, it seems odd.

So great is this method of "retiring" that even employees can do it! Let's pretend you have the typical forty-hour work week in exchange for a paycheck, and you are getting close to retirement age. You and a few neighbors are talking by the fence one morning, steaming mugs in hand, about how all of you have very little saved, and you agree that all of you will most likely have to work until you die. Then, the mailman comes along and starts telling your group of coffee clutchers how he is witnessing a growing opportunity in the trucking industry. He says that one day you will have a new mailman, because his dream is to get into trucking.

One of your neighbors gets a copy of this book and starts talking about it to the other neighbors. Over the next few days, you all discuss the idea and determine that getting a truck good enough to start a trucking business with can be found for only $8,500, while other additional startup costs will run about $2,500. The group decides to approach the mailman and tell him that if he puts in $2,000 to become a one-fifth owner of a new trucking company, the four of you will put in the money needed to get the truck rolling.

For illustration's sake, let's say that the driver (your former mailman) drives five hundred miles a day five days a week, at a profit after expenses (including a bit extra for the driver) of one dollar per mile. That is $10,000 per month in profit. All of the original investment money is paid back, and all four of you in the group have "retirement" paid for, to the tune of $2,000 per month income.

After three months, the group decides to add another driver in order to add even more growth and security. After three more months, you decide to start saving your gravy by investing in other business opportunities that fit in your opportunity basket.

Retirement in this manner allows anyone to catch up. I am often asked how one can catch up to where they believe they should be in terms of saving for retirement. Maybe they are sixty, and don't have two pennies to rub together. Can they still have a wonderful retirement? Absolutely. Maybe it is a couple in their forties, and they recently had to spend some of the nest egg when the husband lost his job a year ago. Can they catch up? Of course. Saving the gravy goes way beyond catching up; it places you in the elite of the elite in terms of those who have the ability to be financially safe and solvent.

Free enterprise, as we discussed, doesn't take a lifetime of compound interest to make a little pile of money, which ends up not being enough. Free enterprise allows you to create a constant flow of income if you choose the right opportunities and spread the action over varying industries. If you plan and invest wisely, your security will be unparalleled.

You Can Also Pass the Gravy

Recently, there were two stories in the news. Both were about little old ladies who had passed away, and each left millions of dollars to charity. When the media addressed these woman's situations, they pointed out that one was a meek secretary, and that the other was a humble teacher. As these two stories grew in the public eye, and as social media drew more and more attention to these stories, it was becoming more obvious that their careers were becoming the focus of the story.

There were comments about how they worked for years and spent wisely. People said that as long as you work hard and save, you can be like these wonderful women. There is no doubt that these women were nice, and they did really give millions of dollars to charity. However, what the media didn't tell people, or at least what they didn't focus on, was where the money they gave away really came from. The media, like the Devil, always uses a grain of truth to make a lie.

In the case of the teacher, her husband started three successful businesses, and he was one of the largest land owners in the county before he died. Upon his death, he left his fortune and his property to his wife, who in turn gave the wealth to charity at the time of her passing.[66] Entrepreneurship provided that money, but the media didn't like that story as much as leading people to believe that a humble profession and wise spending made the charity contributions a reality. The picture of a kind old teacher, feeding her cats, knitting by the window, perhaps sold the story better than, "Successful business owner leaves millions to wife, who leaves millions to charity."

The secretary's story is, you guessed it, very similar. She worked as a secretary for more than forty years, and in one meeting thirty-five years ago, her husband saved a little of their gravy by becoming part owner of a startup business. Over the years, the startup grew into a full-fledged and profitable business. The effort the husband made thirty-five years ago by having a one-hour meeting with the new business owners and deciding to invest produced more income than 83,200 hours of working as a secretary for forty years.[67] Once again, free enterprise empowered her to give away millions of dollars.

It is easy to see that if we are going to age in such a way that enables us to continue God's work, live out our priorities, and truly provide for future generations, then entrepreneurship, or in our case, Evangelpreneurship, should get more attention.

EVANGELPRENEUR ACTION STEP

When we are looking to start our Evangelpreneur careers, we need to ask ourselves what our *why* is, what our vertical alignment is, and how we can design our careers professionally.

The process is similar with retirement, because we really are not retiring at all, but rather transitioning. We need to approach this phase of life not in a manner of slowing down or retreating, but as an opportunity to take advantage of what comes with age—wisdom, patience, and hindsight—as we continue to advance in our walk.

"I have fought a good fight, I have finished my course, I have kept the faith: Henceforth there is laid up for me a crown of righteousness, which the Lord, the righteous judge, shall give me at that day: and not to me only, but unto all them also that love his appearing." —2 Timothy 4:7-8

Take some time and design what you would like to do at this point in your life. Would you like to mentor your grandchildren, or become their homeschool teacher? Perhaps you want to write articles for others in your generation who are facing a scary retirement and doing so with little faith.

Regardless of your current age, think about what you would like to do after you retire. While you are planning your future, start planning what you are going to do with your gravy. Are you going to find an apprentice? Can you begin investing in startups now that fit in your opportunity basket?

It is never too soon or too late to save the gravy. Don't view retirement as the world does; instead, start today by making as many ongoing income streams as possible. Realize that retirement is not something you do when you are done with something else. Rather, realize that the ultimate goal is to gradually work your plan until you are able to fully experience your designed life for the future.

Be careful not to get too excited, though. I have taught this retirement plan to people in the past, and then some invested in twenty businesses in under a month. None fit their opportunity basket, and as a result, they actually spent less time working their vertical alignment.

Money Is a Tool for Salvation

We Are on a Mission: The Number-One Opportunity to Evangelize

WE HAVE A TENDENCY to want to believe that people come to faith because they love God, or because it is the right thing to do. Some people get offended, because they believe that others "use" God by only coming to the faith to avoid Hell. This belief is ridiculous, though, because God Himself says that Salvation is just that: Salvation.

What many believers fail to appreciate is that before a spiritual transformation happens, there is usually an earthly pain that God addresses first. Let's look at some examples from Scripture:

Adam and Eve: They were provided a physical reality with a spiritual foundation. The plants, animals, and even their marriage was provided by God; their physical needs were addressed. Then, the fall of man happened, and God's creation was in need of spiritual salvation. The first thing God addressed was the physical needs of His creation. He took Adam and Eve out of the garden, clothed them, and then provided a system of survival for them. After their physical needs were met, he provided His message of spiritual salvation, outlining it to Adam and Eve, as well as the Devil.

Noah: When God found that Noah was righteous, and determined that He would save Noah from the disaster to come, He did not magically transport him to another realm or supernaturally create the ark. God provided Noah with a physical solution to the problem: the ark. To go even further, God didn't even build the ark for Noah; He still required Noah to do the work.

Joseph: After his brothers sold him into slavery, and he was accused of crimes he didn't commit, God continued to provide for him. God did this by placing Joseph in a position second only to Pharaoh, and then using him to secure food that helped the entire nation withstand the coming drought.

Jesus Met Physical Needs

After the appearance of the Messiah, one would think that the tables would turn—that the storyline would become less about the physical and more about the spiritual aspects, because earthly priorities are no longer very important. However, what we see is exactly the opposite. The first miracle that Yeshua performs is turning water into wine. There wasn't even an overt spiritual message to follow. This serves as a great example of how the Father views the physical as a spiritual expression. We, as humans who desire spiritual closeness, tend to believe that the physical world (needs and joys) are somehow distractions from the spiritual.

The Gospel of Luke shows the Messiah gathering His first disciples. Then, we once again witness the physical need leading the way into the spiritual transformation:

> And he entered into one of the ships, which was Simon's, and prayed him that he would thrust out a little from the land. And he sat down, and taught the people out of the ship.
>
> Now when he had left speaking, he said unto Simon, Launch out into the deep, and let down your nets for a draught.
>
> And Simon answering said unto him, Master, we have toiled all the night, and have taken nothing: nevertheless at thy word I will let down the net.
>
> And when they had this done, they inclosed a great multitude of fishes: and their net brake.
>
> And they beckoned unto their partners, which were in the other ship, that they should come and help them. And they came, and filled both the ships, so that they began to sink.

When Simon Peter saw it, he fell down at Jesus'
knees, saying, Depart from me; for I am a sinful man,
O Lord.

For he was astonished, and all that were with him,
at the draught of the fishes which they had taken:

And so was also James, and John, the sons of
Zebedee, which were partners with Simon. And Jesus
said unto Simon, Fear not; from henceforth thou
shalt catch men.

And when they had brought their ships to land,
they forsook all, and followed him. —Luke 5:3–11

Jesus met their physical needs, and drew in Peter as
well as James and John into His ministry. The soon-
to-be disciples saw their physical problems addressed,
which made them believe in Jesus's spiritual teaching.
In fact, as soon as Peter saw their physical needs met,
he instantly dropped to his knees and gave his life over
to God.

We see the same thing when He fed the masses with
fish and bread. He fed the people, and then addressed the
spiritual by leading people to God.

When He physically healed the leper and the blind
man, these, too, led to the rapid spread of the Gospel.

Another example in which He addressed the physical
before the spiritual is when he told the rich man to give
up his possessions and follow Him.

As a matter of fact, with the exception of Paul, the
physical always seems to be addressed as part of (and

usually before) the spiritual concerns. That is why Jesus Himself said: *"If I have told you earthly things, and ye believe not, how shall ye believe if I tell you of heavenly things?" —John 3:12*

Today's Ailments

In the modern world, it's easy for us to understand this principle on paper. We send food to the poor, help build wells in stricken regions, and supply medical aid to those who need it—all in the name of the Father. We do this without trying to convert people, and yet we still know that it is a part of our faithful ministry; your work helps lead people to Salvation.

What does it say about us, our pride, and our arrogance when we purposely ignore the most important way to bring people of the Western world into the faith?

People ask me why we do not see the miracles in the Western world, when the missionaries in the Third World report miracles regularly. The answer is because physical pain does not plague the Western world. We have the ability now to restore hearing and even sight. We have the ability to make life livable with these and many other afflictions. We have prosthetic devices that move with the user's thoughts and can even feel. As a matter of fact, the current status of prosthetics is no longer about giving someone mobility and capability alone; it is actually going beyond that to aim for superiority—prosthetic limbs that make you run faster and jump higher, and prosthetic arms that allow you to lift and pull more. We have conquered or are in the process of conquering most illnesses. God has blessed the Western world with technology and creativity, while eliminating many worldly pains and obstacles that were so prevalent during Biblical times.

Today, the largest source of stress, struggle, and torment in the lives of people in the Western world, and the largest obstacle to effectiveness in their professional, personal, and spiritual lives, is money. Those in the developed world suffer from:

- Marriages falling apart
- Families falling apart
- Medical problems they cannot afford to treat
- Stress and illness triggered by financial woes
- Not being able to afford quality food for their family

Before a reader assumes incorrectly that this monetary problem is really a problem of greed and excess, I need to point out that not only is that opinion incorrect but even if it were true, it is also completely irrelevant. Why? Because while someone in Canada or Germany may be wealthier than someone living in the Amazon or the Central African Republic, they may still be poor in relation to the culture in which they live. What is even worse is debt, which is unheard of in most poverty-stricken parts of the world, is causing death, homelessness, drug use, and a litany of other problems in the "rich" Western world. As a matter of fact, when the world introduced what is called micro-lending into Third World areas, the introduction of debt actually made things worse and contributed to a rise of suicide because being poor is one thing, but being poor and owing money you cannot pay is even worse. As one report from the Indian state of Andhra Pradesh reported, 70 suicides were reported in 2010 because of the financial stress.[68] In September 2020, *Medical News Today* pointed out that financial hardship is the top risk factor for suicide.[69]

I know this hits home for many of us. I have a member of my team whose father works as a police officer. Prior to the financial hardship caused by the pandemic, the police were being called out to five suicides a week, most of which were financially triggered. During the economic downturn caused by COVID-19, that number grew to five per day!

(D)ebt, which is unheard of in most poverty-stricken parts of the world, is causing death, homelessness, drug use, and a litany of other problems in the "rich" Western world.

These are problems that need real attention. Like it or not, problems with debt have always, and will always, have a negative effect on a Christian's life in the physical world as well as the spiritual. You are not greedy for wanting to free yourself and your family from this bondage.

The reason that the previously mentioned opinion of greed and excess is irrelevant is because while you, a believer, may not place financial woes on your list of concerns, the lost people outside the faith do. This leaves you, the believer, either not connecting the physical to the spiritual in the life of a lost person, or offering the same solution to the lost that the secular world offers them for their problems.

When someone comes to you and your faith to find answers, the answers they seek concern their worldly problems. They don't know enough to even think about spiritual problems. They come to you usually decimated by their problems, often financial ones—if they come to you at all. When a nonbeliever looks at the lives of believers and sees that they have strained relationships caused by money, are in debt for homes and cars, and are taking out loans for degrees they will never use, he doesn't see someone with answers. So why would a nonbeliever listen to a believer about Heavenly things when the *believer* doesn't even understand earthly things?

I am *not* saying that a believer needs to be rich! You do not need $40 million in the bank to have the answers that nonbelievers are looking for; you just need what God wants you to have, which is control over your time and money.

A man or woman who has control over their time and money is so rare these days that finding one is like finding Bigfoot. Those who are not in control of their lives seek control more than anything else, even if they themselves don't always realize it.

When we ignore the calling for us to maintain control over our lives by effectively managing time and resources, then we are missing out on the best way to spread the Good News to the Western world.

As much as we desire spiritual matters to be somehow mythical and supernatural, the reality is that the best way, as Jesus shows us, to lead people to spiritual truth is by addressing their worldly problems with Godly answers.

Jesus, who had little to no money, who had no retirement plan, who had no business to pass along, still knew best when He addressed people's earthly problems first, that by doing so and elevating their physical problems, He captured their attention and trust, and could present a spiritual message. You capture the trust of people in the Western world when they see you effectively managing time and money, because they have a lack of control in those areas. When they see that you, a believer, have answers to the problems they face, they will be open to listening to what you know about the spiritual as well.

EVANGELPRENEUR ACTION STEP

Because being an Evangelpreneur is not about getting rich but rather about how to take control of your time and money, take a moment to identify how having control of time and money would empower you to reach out to a world constantly consumed with money, media, lies, and circumstances. Ask yourself:

- Would you spend more time studying Scripture?
- Would you mentor younger people?
- Would you give more time to outreach?
- Would you develop deeper relationships?
- Would you make the most of the days you have left?

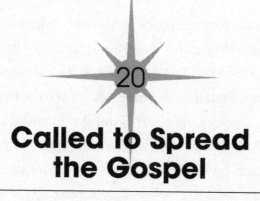

Called to Spread the Gospel

You Are Now an Evangelpreneur

"And he said unto them, Go ye into all the world, and preach the gospel to every creature." —Mark 16:15

T IS TIME TO GET OUT THERE! That vast majority of people reading this book have felt a call to take control of their future through entrepreneurship. Now that you know how powerful the Evangelpreneur is in spreading the Gospel, it is obviously time to become not only an entrepreneur but an Evangelpreneur. This is someone who lives out their faith and is no longer controlled by money, who uses the marketplace to go beyond a simple marketplace ministry and to a level of marketplace evangelism.

Is being an Evangelpreneur the only way to spread the Gospel? No. While this chapter is specifically for those who have made the decision to become Evangelpreneurs, I also want to encourage those who make the decision not to become Evangelpreneurs. I believe in you, I encourage you, and I also hope that you understand the power that free enterprise will give you. It is my desire that you, as a non-Evangelpreneur, will support business owners who are Evangelpreneurs!

I remember having dinner with the president of the Charlotte Christian Chamber of Commerce, and he was telling me that a dollar spent in an Islamic business will be re-spent in that community over two dozen times before it leaves that community. Similarly, he told me that a dollar spent in a Jewish business will be re-spent in that community over a dozen times. When it came to Christian spending and support, however, a dollar would be spent only once in a Christian business before it leaves the community and enters the secular marketplace.

In a very impromptu and nonscientific survey I conducted outside a church where I was speaking, I asked about fifty people how often they make a point of spending money with businesses who share their faith. With the exception of bookstores and coffee shops, the most common answer was "Well, I don't think about that," or "I usually just find the lowest price because I'm trying to be a good steward." However, I would argue that "being a good steward" doesn't mean always finding the lowest price.

The importance of supporting businesses that are operated by people who share your faith is vital to the spread of the Gospel. Let me tell you something that you may find shocking. Every church west of Jamestown is the result of entrepreneurship! After people settled Jamestown, people left because they wanted to trap, log, find gold, or what have you. When a number of entrepreneur loggers would set up a base camp, other entrepreneurs came along and offered services such as food, bathing, clothing and tool repair, and supplies. The camp would grow to a small town. Eventually, a pastor would realize that in this entrepreneur development deep in the woods, there were dozens of people who needed spiritual leadership.

This isn't limited to church expansion, either. The reason there are hospitals, schools, and parks in any town west of the East Coast is because of entrepreneurship. We don't teach that fact today, partially because people don't even realize it. It is time we, as believers, understand that entrepreneurship is important. David, Solomon, Peter, Paul, Abraham, Moses, and pretty much every other figure in the Scriptures was an entrepreneur. Even if you choose not to be, support those who are, teach it as an option to your children, and promote the expansion of it to those in your church.

As Evangelpreneurs, there are many ways to serve that will accomplish mixing your faith with your entrepreneurship, and we will examine a few of them here.

Direct Exposure

This is your daily opportunity. In the course of your business, you should not hide the fact that you are a believer in God. Placing a Scripture verse on the outside of every customer's bag or on the bottom of a receipt are good examples of direct exposure. If applicable, integrate faith-themed products into your product line. There are so many ways to do this, so really let your imagination soar. However, the most important point is that you are incorporating your faith in your day-to-day business operations.

Funding Message Expansion

Planting seeds and spreading the Gospel: that is the goal, right? Funding message expansion is how the Word moves throughout the world. Many pastors will tell you that the one who sends the missionary will get the same reward in Heaven as the missionary himself. This should be a fundamental part of your Evangelpreneur plan.

You can work this into your operation in a number of ways. The simplest is to take money off the top and give it to a missionary or missionary organization. This has a tendency to be inconsistent though, because it is common for costs, expansion, debt, or a million other reasons to prevent you from giving a consistent amount.

A better plan would be something like this: Take one day every other week, and give the revenue you generate on that day directly to the mission effort. Pick the day, make it consistent, and make sure you have the day picked prior to calculating the giving. Don't cheat and say, "I will give one day a month to mission funding," and then go over the books and pick a day on which your business generated little revenue.

If the day you pick (e.g., every other Tuesday) happens to draw high proceeds, then so be it. After all, maybe God made that day profitable to see if you are a person of your word and faith!

That's just one idea, of course, but I strongly suggest that if this is how you are going to use Evangelpreneurship, do not calculate a number to give to missions at the end of the month. More often than not, if you wait until the end of the month, there will be months when you give nothing at all. Besides, when you actually make it a part of your operation, you get more involved, excited, and rewarded by the experience. If you have a retail location, you could even do something as simple as selling one unique product, and giving 100 percent of the profits from that product to mission work.

Sponsoring Transformation

There needs to be much more transformation sponsorship. People grow and change through experiences. Someone's first concert could set them on the road to a career in music. Witnessing a terror attack could lead someone to enlist in the armed services. The first walk up the ramp into a Major League ballpark is a memory fathers and sons continue to hold as a bond decades later. Experiences change and mold us, and if you really think about it, life is just a journey full of experiences.

The same holds true for faith. When we look at the Bible, do we find that the disciples left tracts (Bible verses) on doorposts at night? No, the opposite is actually true; what we find is that the entirety of Scripture is experiences. Every single book, even books like Leviticus and Deuteronomy (which many believe only concern laws and rules), profiles experiences.

In a more modern sense, how many millions came to faith through revival meetings, where hundreds if not thousands of people fill tents and arenas? How many people like a song such as "I Can Only Imagine" by MercyMe, for example, not knowing that it is a song of faith the first time they hear it? The fourth time they hear it, they tell everyone how it is their new favorite song, and by the time MercyMe has a concert in the area, that person finds themselves at a religious event hearing a message they never heard before.

The point is this: Experiences work. As Evangelpreneurs, we need to look at ways to facilitate more experiences.

Concerts, speaking events, even sporting events in which church teams interact with secular teams, are all great opportunities to use events to expand the reach of the Word. I have been in cities where there are church softball leagues, and there are as many as twelve or fifteen teams. They play each other as a way to build church-to-church relationships, and that is fine. However, what if once a summer they hosted "The Mother of All Softball Tournaments?" Over the course of a Friday night, Saturday, and Sunday, they invite all of the softball teams in town to participate. On Sunday morning, they could hold church right there in the stands (attended by members of secular teams), and of course there is opportunity for one-on-one connection as well. Every game could start with a quick prayer, and the awards ceremony for the tournament would obviously happen in one of the participating churches.

Getting involved as an Evangelpreneur in events such as this one can take many forms. Sponsorship of more events is desperately needed, so if you have a level of success, you can help in this regard. Currently, there are too few sponsored events, and the ones that are happening seem to focus on marketing to Christians only. You can change that so there is outreach beyond the choir, so to speak.

If you are not yet at a level to financially contribute to sponsoring events, you can organize or promote them. Taking those skills that so few have and applying them to events not only accomplishes the mission of the event but also enables you to hone your skills. Additionally, you can be an example to those around you of someone who knows business, how to get things done in a community, and lives out their faith.

Freedom to Testify

The fact that Evangelpreneurship gives you more control over time and money allows you to give your testimony more readily. In addition, as a pillar of a community, people are interested in hearing your testimony. Right or wrong, the truth of the matter is that when people look for someone to speak, they usually want someone of prominence or success. We could argue for days on how every voice is just as valid, and I agree, but if you are going to spread the Gospel to a secular culture, then you need to realize the truths that operate in that culture.

There is not much to go into depth on for this particular point other than a willingness to seek out opportunities to present your testimony. Recognize that you may have more freedom in terms of time after you become an Evangelpreneur than you had before you read this book.

Life Example

This is the best tool for leading people to faith, because opportunities are present every day. It also has the most criticism attached to it.

You have probably heard the term "lifestyle evangelism" or "lifestyle ministry." These terms are often seen as negative, because people believe they simply describe people that are braggadocios. Sadly, that is usually the case.

We see many people of faith who are in the public eye who have the Rolls-Royce, the Patek Phillipe watch, and the McMansion. They claim it is all part of living in the "glory," and that their life serves as a way to use "lifestyle evangelism" to lead people to God. They do lead people to *a* god—I'm just not sure which god.

Before you know it, a news story breaks that reveals that they are in a sex scandal, beat their wife or kid, or somehow money has gone missing.

Now, let me say that whether rich or poor, we all sin. However, we can all repent and experience restoration.

The larger point I'm making is that those people who use only wealth to claim "lifestyle evangelism" missed the lifestyle part.

There is a place for lifestyle evangelism. The Messiah, Peter, Paul, David, Abraham, and Solomon all practiced real lifestyle evangelism. For example, Yeshua kept the Torah (the first five books of the Bible; the word means "instruction"), which drew people who kept Torah to the realization that He indeed was the Word made flesh. David used his wealth to build a temple to Elohim, as did Solomon. Abraham walked in obedience and became the first Hebrew (one who has crossed over), which drew followers to him based on his example alone.

The key to making it work is completeness. Does your lifestyle with your wife serve as an example of a Godly marriage? Does your lifestyle with your kids show the Biblical definition of raising children as well as love? Does your lifestyle include the study and proclamation of the Word? Does your lifestyle in your community reflect that you are a representative of the Most High through your service to those who live in your area? Does your lifestyle in terms of your health serve as an example of how you treat God's creation?

And yes, does your lifestyle in your finances resemble a child of God who understands how to make, spend, and steward money in a Godly way as part of the marketplace? Lifestyle evangelism is, or should be, an example of having and working your vertical alignment. When we look closely at those who seem to use this form of "lifestyle evangelism" today, we don't see an alignment that lines up with what they say. Is God on their alignment? Sure, and they will tell you He is number one; but in reality, He is number five.

Even though you may fail to live out your alignment at times, if you have it in the right order, real restoration and success in life as a whole is possible. Even that process of restoration, if you are engaged in the proper form of lifestyle evangelism, will serve as a lifestyle example!

"Ye shall know them by their fruits. Do men gather grapes of thorns, or figs of thistles? Even so every good tree bringeth forth good fruit; but a corrupt tree bringeth forth evil fruit. A good tree cannot bring forth evil fruit, neither can a corrupt tree bring forth good fruit." —Matthew 7:16–18

A relationship with God grows "good fruit." God wants you to have a good relationship with your spouse. God says that raising your children in His ways is good. God also, to the shock of some pastors, considers financial empowerment a "good fruit," as we have discovered beyond the shadow of a doubt in this book.

What does this all mean? It means that if you drive to church in a nice car, and in that car is a wife you serve as Christ served the church, and in her hand is the hand of a little one whom you raise according to God's will, then you are a great example. If on the way to church, you anonymously gave a meal and a tract to a homeless man, then you yield good fruit. You don't need to feel bad or guilty about the nice car. You know you are no better or worse than the older man who had to take the bus to church. But that situation is also why you are working on securing a church bus to bring your equal brothers and sisters to church.

The truth behind lifestyle evangelism and the misconception about its relation to wealth is twofold. Not only are there people who essentially abuse wealth—and we all can name a few—but there are also people who don't have wealth, and justify their envy by claiming righteousness. Envy in the church is when someone who doesn't have what they want in life (money, spouse, health, etc.) claims that when others have those things, they have made those things idols, and their priorities out of order. It is easy to find a verse or a church that will allow you to hide envy, and empower you to lie to yourself and others.

Instead, what you should be doing is giving thanks for every breath you have, because one breath is more valuable than all the treasures on earth. You should also see those who have success as an example. More often than not, when you dig a bit deeper into the lives of those who hide their envy in a Bible, they once had dreams of success, but failed. The bitterness of their failure and the death of a dream can create a cynical person. If you are that person, pray that God corrects your path, and that He reveals to you that it is never too late to achieve success in any area of life. While you are at it, pray that God puts an Evangelpreneur and mentor in your life to serve as an example as you move forward with your renewed and corrected view on life.

EVANGELPRENEUR ACTION STEP

There really is no step associated with this chapter, because if you do the rest of what the book teaches, this chapter will take care of itself. If I had to give an action step to go along with what you learned in this chapter, I would instruct you to place yourself in positions in which you are humbled (not embarrassed or abused), and reminded that what you have or do not have is fleeting, and that life is precious. You are, even with any success you may achieve in life, just dust. If it was not for the divine spark placed inside you, you would have nothing, be nothing, and possess no promise of a future.

I would also suggest that you embrace the reality that you are wrong at times. Admitting that you are wrong is one of the hardest things for many of us. However, if we are never wrong, how can we ever learn and grow?

People assume that because I have a life that is more public than that of others, I must believe I'm right all of the time. The truth of the matter is that I have developed a desire to be wrong. I admit, realizing I'm incorrect initially results in an internal moment of pride and resistance, but I know that I would rather win in the end than be ignorant of my failings.

Embrace the reality that you are wrong and listen to people who show you why you are wrong. Those who do so with aggression or attitude are not worth your time. Could they be correct? Sure, but their stupidity and immaturity prevent anyone from being able to realize the truth of their message. Ironically, those who want to prove you wrong, as opposed to educate you and lift you up, are wrong in what they are doing. By their poor approach of aggressiveness and a bad attitude, they are becoming the very thing they are supposedly fighting against. I call those people "silly grown children," and remind them often to put their big-boy pants back on.

PART 5

Doing Church

The New You
in Your Old Church

Being an Evangelpreneur
in an Employment Church

WHETHER YOU ATTEND a small church in someone's home, or attend a modern church building, you will be among your fellow believers. The difference is, now that you have been exposed to Bible-based teaching that has been previously ignored, you will feel like you know something that everyone else seems to have missed. The truth is, after reading this book, you now know what others don't and will want to share with all of your fellow believers the dynamic change you have experienced.

I remember a roommate I had a long time ago who became a new believer. He would go out and spread a fire-and-brimstone message to everyone. I remember that for a while he would go out at night to the bars he used to hang out in, and go right up to his old drinking buddies and tell them, "You are about to go to Hell, you need Jesus right now, and I can lead you in the prayer."

This might come as a shock, but not a single one of those old drinking buddies came to the faith on those occasions. Honestly, his manner of evangelism left such a sour taste that for years it prevented them from being open to hearing the message of the Gospel. It is not that my roommate was wrong. There is a time and a place for the fire-and-brimstone speech; however, his method of delivery shut down his intended audience before they could even consider his comments.

The same phenomenon happens when you finish this book. You may say, "They are greedy, they love money when they say they don't, and they should not go to work on Monday." You will want to run up to every fellow believer and tell them that they are all wrong.

DO NOT DO THAT!

In this chapter, we will forgo the Evangelpreneur Action Step, because the whole chapter is basically the outline of the steps. We will examine the proper way of taking what you have just learned and sharing it with your fellow believers.

Don't Condemn

Look, I know that at certain points in the book I am blunt—very blunt. At no time do I intend to condemn or offend the reader personally. As a matter of fact, if you feel that way, I apologize. There is a reason for my tone in this book. I prefer to be brutally blunt because the lies I expose are so fortified that it takes a heavy hammer to break through them. I teach not from the perspective of a mother rearing little ones, but as a drill instructor getting grown adults over the obstacles. When it comes to addressing masses (like in a book, on the radio, or at a large speaking event), the presenter, in this case me, can be more abrasive with an audience to get a point across and make people think, because the audience does not tend to take the message as a personal attack. When addressing a small group of people, or an individual, bluntness is not the way to go. In face-to-face exchanges, the audience tends to take things personally. This effect is magnified if you are addressing people you personally know.

When you are talking to people you know, they will perceive your bluntness as you showing off how much you know, and friends and family don't like that much. Even if your intentions are to prove them wrong in an effort to get them on the right track, you may actually prevent them from being receptive to the message you are trying to give. Be soft, tender, and patient.

How to Effectively Share

There is an expression I find absolutely annoying: "You can lead a horse to water, but you can't make him drink." The reason I find this expression so annoying is because it is not at all true. Of course you can make a horse drink; you just need to make him thirsty first.

When you approach someone who has a contrary point of view from the one you desire to share, the intended recipient typically rejects, let alone rationally considers, the new information before it is even presented. If you are close with someone, the effect is multiplied. For example, if you are married and you try to tell your spouse something, say on a political topic, they will usually reject the new stance, especially if it is contrary to how the two of you viewed the issue before. Then, weeks or months later, they will come home from work and present the idea to *you* as if they came up with it, and they now want you to believe it. This of course leaves you scratching your head, and feeling like you are not heard by your own spouse. I have an entire lesson on why that happens and how to overcome it, but for the sake of our conversation, suffice it to say that force-feeding new ideas to people usually meets objection. Hence the expression, "You can lead a horse to water but you can't make him drink."

So, how do we change the odds of the horse drinking? How do we get him thirsty first? You do so by asking for help.

You need to decide, is your intention really to change a person? Or is your intention to get credit for being the man or woman who brought this new information to your congregation, family, or culture? If the objective is to really effect change, then we need to put aside ego and pride, and go for the win.

By asking the people close to you for help, you are flattering them by letting them know you value their input and wisdom; preventing rejection before they even consider the new information; and involving them in the discovery, which has long-term benefits.

It could be something simple: "Hey guys, in my Bible study I just read this book *Evangelpreneur*, and the author really makes a lot of sense that I didn't see before I read it. I really value your opinion and was hoping you could help me out. Before I do what the author says to do, I would love to hear what you have to say. Can you read this and just tell me, yes or no, does he make sense?"

A word of caution: Someone may read this book and then, due to pride or misunderstanding, tell you that this is all wrong. He may tell you that working at your current job, leveraging your debt, and increasing your tithe is all you need to do, and that by reading this book, you are becoming greedy. If that happens, first tell that person that I would love for them to call my show, *The Josh Tolley Show*, and talk to me about their position. Second, you are responsible for your own decisions. You need to use logic, reason, and strategy to assess what I have presented here. If your logic and reason are sound, you will more than likely find that this book is right, and that you and your family should take the suggested actions. This leads us to the next point.

Actions Speak Louder than Words

At some point after reading this book (and attending one of my training events), you need to walk the walk. You need to be an example of an actual Evangelpreneur. This of course includes taking advantage of free enterprise as a revenue-generating machine for you and your family, but it means more than that. Becoming an example includes becoming the customer of other faith-based businesses and promoting them to your fellow congregants, and even helping the church leadership generate revenue and eliminate debt. Get involved in fund-raising events, and run them not with the employee mind-set, which you may have done in the past, but with the creativity and understanding of an Evangelpreneur.

Sometimes Their Words
Are Louder Than Your Actions

Sometimes, people who are supposed to uplift and encourage you actually offer only insults and discouragement. They tell you that you could start a business and fail, you could try to help a fellow business owner and fail, you could give someone this book to read and perhaps they don't like that the author is a ginger (by the way, only a ginger can call another ginger a ginger)...the list of possibilities are endless. Then, you will find out who the real black-hearted "followers of Jesus" are. I remember a buddy of mine with whom I went to church started a business (this was way before I started doing any training), and his business failed. The first day back in church, people who "supported" him were telling him that he needed to get a "real job" and get his head out of the clouds. They told him that he didn't have the right educational training, and that the economy just wasn't right for business at the time. He then told these people that he was going to start another business, and the responses were, "You are chasing money and greed" and "Just follow the Lord and let Him provide."

It's funny that when a member of the congregation was struggling to make ends meet and got a part-time job, that person wasn't "chasing money." Why do we pay the pastor, or the contractor who built the building? Shouldn't they "just follow the Lord and let Him provide?" Why didn't the congregation of several hundred, instead of watching my buddy fail, come together in support of a brother in Christ and become customers?

What you will find more often than not is that a fairly large segment of any congregation masks their jealousy and fear behind false righteousness and a couple out-of-context verses. I wish we could just say to all these evildoers, "Get behind me, HaSatan," but that doesn't go over too well. They can tell you that you are greedy, even though you want free enterprise to put food on the table and help missionaries in the field, but Heaven forbid you point out their evil hypocrisy.

Don't let them get to you. You can refer to them as Judas, as Yeshua did to Thomas, who was consumed with unfaithful doubt. Refer to them that way privately, of course. However, do not let them stop you. Yes, you could fail, but what a great example you are to everyone else when you act in faith and get back up and try again. We don't write books or watch movies with people who give up—nor does YHVH fill Scripture with such individuals—but He does fill His Word with those who failed and got back up.

Could you imagine how boring a baseball game would be if after the first strikeout, the players all went back inside the clubhouse, because the first attempt failed? How lonely would the world be if men stopped asking women out after the first one rejects them? How few real believers would exist in the world if people stopped sharing the Gospel after one failed attempt?

Lead a Study

I remember going to many Wednesday night meetings and reading books like *The Purpose Driven Life*, or *The Total Money Makeover*, and other popular books sold at the local Christian bookstore. Some of the books were better than others, but the conversations were always great.

Make my book the next book on your group list. If your congregation is dedicated to prayer and Scripture on Wednesday, that's awesome and I support that. However, that doesn't mean you cannot have a study group based around this book on Thursday, or meet up with other believers after church on Saturday or Sunday. Yes, I would enjoy selling books, but that is not really the intention. If people can't afford the books, then share one copy. The intention is to get people back to a place where they understand and practice a method of economic operation, which is Biblical and sound.

By the time you finish this copy, there will undoubtedly be a calling for a church study program based on this book, so I will do my part by continuing to provide resources on the individual and corporate level.

Mugging the Woman with Two Coins

A Message to Church Leadership

N THE BOOK OF LUKE (Luke 21:1–4) we see the following example:

> And he looked up, and saw the rich men casting their gifts into the treasury.
>
> And he saw also a certain poor widow casting in thither two mites.
>
> And he said, Of a truth I say unto you, that this poor widow hath cast in more than they all:
>
> For all these have of their abundance cast in unto the offerings of God: but she of her penury hath cast in all the living that she had.

Churches across the Western world ignorantly use this woman's tale as a message to teach giving, and to encourage tithing. The truth is, we cannot point to this woman and then to the faithful and say, "Be as this woman. Even if you don't have much, you can give what little you have."

It alarms me that the audacity and arrogance of churches results in them asking for and accepting money, yet they do not Biblically teach how to make that money, or how to use that money once it is earned. The understanding and application of this verse is a great example of how many churches miss the real point.

In the era of this woman, there was "debtor's jail." It was a punishment system that locked up someone in debt. Knowing that, what do we know about this woman? We know that while she might be poor, she was not in debt; if she were, she would be in jail and unable to provide this powerful message in the Scripture.

What we are doing as believers (and church leaders) is essentially mugging this woman for her story, and stealing the power behind the teaching.

Today, we will go into a church and hear someone teach, using this woman as an example. After the service, though, we teach our children to get student loans, and we get auto loans and mortgages we cannot really afford. The church now even accepts credit cards so you can "give freely."

As leaders in faith, I understand the desire to want to do things correctly and lead people to a relationship with God. The intent and heart are most likely in the right place. Please understand that by teaching that money isn't important, and teaching that money is the root of all evil, evil actually gets a foothold. When the people need answers and churches give only things like "get out of debt, give to the local storehouse, and be a good steward," then those people are going to go looking for answers elsewhere.

When the lost turn to God's children for answers in an area of life, and God's children do not know how to address an issue (even though God does), the lost don't believe that the children know what they are talking about on any issue.

After reading this book, you, as church leadership, are really left with two options:

1. You can try to discredit this book as false, teaching greed, or "prosperity gospel." This of course would be wrong, and I think you know that.

2. You could realize that the teaching in this book does have a place, and should be taught, as it does not take away from the message of God's love and His Salvation. Rather, it puts God and His teaching back in the daily lives of those who implement the practices presented herein. (I do not blame churches for not teaching what should be taught. How do you teach that which you do not know is available?)

If you decide to go with the first option, then I would strongly encourage you to call into my show, *The Josh Tolley Show* (find out more at JoshTolley.com). I would love to talk to you. There are too many "Christians" who post nasty comments online or spread criticism in other ways. I'm so appalled by shallow pastors and believers taking to the Net to "expose" something or someone. All they are really exposing is that they don't know how they are supposed to act as adult Christians. My recommendation to you would be that before you start posting and talking, reach out to me and prove that I'm incorrect. As someone who believes in God and accepts His Son as my Lord and Savior, I would appreciate your calling and demonstrating a more appropriate action by lovingly correcting my possible misunderstanding, realizing that we both want the same thing. Admittedly, few people will choose the first option, and most will go with the second. After reading this book, you are now on the right track. I would like to continue to help. I would gladly work with your church to train and equip leaders to teach Evangelpreneurship, as well as members who are looking to become Evangelpreneurs.

A church that has set its vertical alignment, knows how to work that alignment, and treats enterprise as a vital part of a knitted culture of believers is a powerful church.

Conclusion

IFE IS A JOURNEY, not a destination. When you reach the end of a road trip and the vacation is over, the experiences along the journey always prove more memorable than the destination itself. Somehow, when you do get there, all of the obstacles, breakdowns, or odd things that happened along the way result in a greater appreciation of your arrival.

The same is true with life. When you talk to a couple that has been married for decades, or friends who have known each other since childhood, the stories that get the most smiles are the ones of overcoming something together.

When you are going through a challenge, you often don't see it that way. A flat tire can ruin a day, and a speeding ticket can set you off on those around you for the next three hundred miles. Isn't it funny how the bad things become the memorable things when you get to your destination?

In life and business, we see the same thing. We see the challenges and the failures, and think that they ruin the trip. However, just as when you are on vacation, the problems become the points that truly make you who you are, and what fuel your success.

Does anyone ever read a book or watch a movie about someone who didn't have to overcome an obstacle? Does the Bible have any examples of people who were born, lived a life of no challenges, and experienced no problems? Even the Messiah Himself faced challenges. The glory of the story comes from overcoming death, and saving Creation from destruction.

We need to take a different look at failure, then, when we look at business. Failure is the sign of real effort, and the indicator that there is an opportunity to grow. Too often, we let pride influence how we experience and react to failure, which leads to quitting or shame.

As a quick note, I know that not everyone in your life will support your pursuits of Evangelpreneurship. These people will lie in wait for you to fail, and when you do, they will spare no time pointing it out. Anyone who points out your failure to discourage you from trying again, or to imply that you are not ready to succeed, is someone who not only has not accomplished anything of merit in their life, but is spewing evil, regardless of how many times they say, "Bless your heart."

Obviously, God is all you need to see you through and prayer will do more than my words on paper. However, I want to take a moment and personally encourage you.

You are at a fork in the road. One option is, you can ignore what you just read and go on living the same way. But choose that route with this word of warning: The seed has been planted, and you know as well as I do that what has been said in this book is true. Because of that, if you do try to ignore this book, the seed of hope and dreams will grow in your heart and mind anyway, to the point where the pain of fighting against doing what you know you should causes so much pain you will wish you never read this book. Five years might go by and your life may not change much. But, before you know it, you will get laid off, and your wife will have an operation that insurance won't cover, and this book will come back to your mind, but by then it may be too late.

The other option is to move forward. Recognize that there has always been a divine spark in you, and this book seemed to pour fuel all over it. Your life seems to be clearer. You always knew you were created to have a relationship with God, but you know that He wants you to be a good steward of that life, and now you know how.

For you, my words of encouragement are to do what is outlined in the book. Between the instructional information found in each chapter and the Evangelpreneur Action Steps, this will prepare the runway for takeoff.

Don't stop there. Do yourself a favor, and continue to study and grow. Just as you always grow in the Word, you can always grow in life. And since being an Evangelpreneur is really about success in life as a whole, you can never stop learning.

I offer training and events and I strongly urge you to attend them. More importantly, though, I want you to understand what Evangelpreneurship is, how powerful it is for spreading the Gospel, and how free enterprise is the fuel for freedom. Those things are more important than attending my events, so even if it is not me who trains you, get training from another trusted and qualified source!

I will end with this: There will be those who discourage you. At times, that person may even be yourself. Fear not, because you can do all things through the One who saved you.* When God is with you, who can be against you?**

---

* Phillippians 4:13
** Romans 8:31

FAQ

Read Them!

Josh, what about regulation? Isn't regulation making it hard to start businesses?

Regulation is a problem; there is no doubt about it. The fact that regulation is passed to make it harder for people to engage in free enterprise should be a red flag to you. The excuse of "consumer protection" is used by regulatory bodies to prevent business from growing around the world and in many industries. A perfect example of that is the taxi business in New York City. To protect the customer, the city only allows so many taxis to operate, and to be one of the lucky taxi owners you need to have the city-issued medallion. Well, this comes with a price, of course, and in 2013 the price of one medallion was $1.25 million.[70] Does this amount of money make the taxi safer for the customer? Of course not. Does it benefit the customer in any way? Of course not. As a matter of fact, it increases their costs because the driver has to pay the $1.25 million expense up front. And it doesn't make the rider safer, as the million-plus dollars spent on regulation could have gone to improved safety equipment. So what does this really accomplish, then? It keeps the little guy out of the game. It allows the big-money players with political connections to dominate the market without worry of the small guy coming in and taking away business. Regulation also exposes fascists working within governments, because we see industries in bed with political operatives, which creates an environment that limits competition from entering the marketplace. Everything from medical treatments to transportation services are closed to new competition because of the growth of fascism.

With that said, so what? Your options are employment or entrepreneurship. Regulation or not, entrepreneurship is the only option that gives you control of your future. We need to be strategic in our positioning when starting a business. Let's assume you want to start a taxi company in New York, but because of regulation, it costs you $1 million to start and that is an amount that you just don't have. If your dream is to still have a cab company in NYC, perhaps starting a cab company in upstate New York for a tenth of the price, and working your way up from one cab will place you in a better position. If you are smart and progress wisely, you most likely will have the $1 million available to move into the city after five years.

Regulation should never stop you from becoming an entrepreneur; it should separate those small businesses that don't have a strategic skill set from those that do. Remember, more entrepreneurs becoming successful is how we actually destroy much of that regulation, as entrepreneurs become more politically active and able to support candidates to repeal laws currently on the books (or run for office themselves), reopen the markets by creative circumvention, and even establish new areas of business where the politicians have not yet used their pen to stifle entrepreneurship.

In this bad economy, is now really the best time to start a business?

Yes. To start this answer, we need to go back to the previous question and see that you have two options: employment or entrepreneurship. In a bad economy with downsizing, layoffs, outsourcing, and a weakened dollar, why on earth would you ever want to be in a place where you have no control, when the economy is so terrible? We need to reverse the question and ask those who object to starting a business, "In this bad economy, is now really the time to hand over control of your capability to produce income to a boss who you don't know, would fire you if needed, and doesn't care as much about your family as you do?"

We also have to look at practicality. When you look back over history, we see great amounts of wealth created during poor economic times. In some ways, the bad times are better than the good times for entrepreneurship, because bad times allow you to do things that would not be possible during good times.

For example, in good times, rental requirements for commercial space may be $10 per square foot and a five-year lease. On a small location of only 1,000 square feet, you are looking at a cost of $10,000 per month. This is a huge expense for most startup businesses. By contrast, in a bad economy, when buildings are sitting empty, a deal on the same space could be a one-year lease with the first two months free, and $3 per square foot. You can find similar opportunities with suppliers who need to lower their prices to stay in business, and who have accumulating assets—for example, an equipment dealer cannot afford to sit on inventory for months like it could in the good times.

Bad economic times actually allow the little guy to compete with the big guy, and allow a transfer of market share from the big guys to the little guys, which isn't as easy when times are good.

Sure, there are advantages to having money in bad times and having money in good times. Having money is never a bad thing. Maybe the money you had during the good times that you could have used to start a business has diminished now that the economy is not at its peak, which puts more strain on what little you have to use for a startup. The facts don't change, though, and the fact is that any economic condition holds opportunity and, yes, those opportunities can vary greatly from time to time based on how your personal financial condition relates to the financial conditions surrounding you.

Therefore, the best time to start a business is now, regardless of when "now" is. Good times and bad times shouldn't matter to an Evangelpreneur with training.

My pastor tells me that pursuing wealth is a sin; I don't feel like that's true and your book makes sense. What do I do?

I would start by giving this book to your pastor and giving him the opportunity to learn what you just learned. Hopefully, that ends the problem for you.

Unfortunately, that will not work with all pastors. The reason that pastors feel pursuing wealth is a sin is either because they have pride of what they believe is sound judgment, or they have an improper understanding of Scripture.

Nowhere in the Bible is a wealthy person called a sinner because they are wealthy. If your life belongs to God, if your vertical alignment is sound and being lived out, then wealth is the natural result of working to the strengths of your

God-given abilities. Would a pastor not want you to do your best in your career? Would a pastor want you to give poor customer service, because customers were referring too many people to your business? Would a pastor not want you to employ the new believer in church who just kicked a drug habit? Does the pastor not believe 2 Thessalonians 3:10, which says that if a man chooses not to work, he shall not eat? If he does believe it, does he believe a man shouldn't do a good job? I would suggest reading my answer to the question later in this FAQ concerning the rich man and the camel getting through the eye of a needle.

If I could run a seminary, I would require that each student spend at least one year as an entrepreneur. It would expose to pastors what entrepreneurship really is, and how God created the first entrepreneur when he created Adam. If your pastor believes that wanting to be successful in business is pursuing wealth, the pastor usually doesn't understand what you are really pursuing, and is confused.

I am on board 100 percent with what you are saying, and I can feel the pull in my heart to be an Evangelpreneur. My wife, on the other hand, does not agree. What do I do?

Love is patient, kind, slow to anger, and quick to forgive. It is important to point out that your marriage is much more important than this book or some business. With that said, this book and a business run by a trained Evangelpreneur can save and grow a marriage.

My first suggestion would be to read this book with her. The interesting thing about a spouse is that they are the one person with whom you are supposed to feel the safest, and that safety extends to things you believe. Because of this, spouses need to communicate in such a way that allows beliefs to grow without feeling attacked. I teach on this, and I would highly recommend that any married couple attend any of my events as a couple.

Without getting too deep, the power behind reading it with her is *not* so you can tell her what you believe at the end of every chapter, or to express your opinion on every chapter. The purpose of reading it with her is to allow her to speak. You may not like what she has to say at the end of a chapter, and she may not like me because she doesn't like red beards or what have you. If you are patient with her, you will hear her beliefs and exactly why she is opposed to advancing with your Evangelpreneur goals.

What you will most likely find is that her fear comes from a place of risk to her and the family's security. The best way to address this is to work with her over the course of a weekend to develop your vertical alignment and your list of *why*s. When that has been done, both of you will soon find that employment does not afford the freedom to do your best in many areas of life.

At that point, it would be a good opportunity to read-dress the issue, and suggest that she brainstorm with you on what sort of starter business you could begin on a part-time basis, posing very little risk to the family.

I have bad credit and spent five years in prison. Can I still become an Evangelpreneur?

Yale or jail, it makes no difference. The great thing about Evangelpreneurship is that race, sex, faith, and even history are things that should not stop anyone from pursuing their Evangelpreneur goals.

Many people believe that their past limits them. We have all fallen, including me, and your failures build you into the strong person you are meant to be. I remember days that seem like yesterday; I was borrowing money and going to collections court. Looking back on those days, my challenges gave me the foundation, wisdom, and motivation to accomplish what I am doing today. I can say with confidence that I will fail in the future as well, as will everyone who is reading these words. When the past is fresh, it can seem intimidating. But when you progress in your walk, past challenges and failures become things for which you actually become thankful. People who don't understand that or constantly bring up your past are evil, soulless liars, and suffering from denial.

To be honest, the success stories I like the most, the success stories we write books and make movies about, are the ones that include the most past failures. There are not many movies about a young man who grew up, made no mistakes, graduated, and inherited Dad's business with no failures or challenges.

We can even look to our faith to prove this point. The fact that we are sinners saved by grace makes Salvation so powerful. If there were no sin to conquer, there would be no need for the greatest events in human history: Creation, Fall, Salvation, and Resurrection.

I'm assuming you have repented for your sins, have done your best to make restitution for those wronged, and have accepted the cleansing gift of Salvation. If so, you are as white as snow, my friend. Go forth and write your future.

What about tithing?

This is a great question. It is almost impossible to talk about money in the context of faith and not encounter the issue of tithes and offerings. I purposely did not write a chapter addressing this topic, because I didn't want the topic to overshadow the teaching presented. That is not to say that the issue of tithes and offerings is not important—it is. What I cover in this book does not violate any doctrinal position of any denomination, or faith for that matter; it exposes the truth regarding how we are to earn our money, and our approach to money as a whole.

Tithes and offerings are a bit different, because different faiths and denominations have varying doctrinal positions. Since I don't believe we all need to agree on the specifics of tithes and offerings in order to be saved, I did not want to fuel an argument that might distract from the important teaching contained in this book. Perhaps in the future, I will teach on the tithing issue, but now is not that time.

You seem pretty opposed to what are considered financial products: 401(k)s, mutual funds, stocks, CDs, etc. Are they really that bad, and are you really that opposed to them?

If someone has one of these financial products, I'm not going to look down on them. If someone sells these products, I don't hate them or think they are evil just because they sell these products. If you have money, it is yours, and you are free to do what you wish with it. God gives you free will, and I will not pass judgment on you as a person even though I may have a judgment on the product.

I will say this: The more I learned about Wall Street–based products, and the more I learned that Wall Street cannot really provide true and effective compounding interest, the more I avoided them. The more I learned we were all lied to about "buy term and invest the difference," the more I started finding and offering alternative solutions.

Today I focus on teaching people to protect their money first (which cannot be done with a Wall Street–based product) and then finding Evangelpreneurship options that produce much better returns. (For more information about how to protect your money, go to www.Shyft-Capital.com.)

The larger point that I'm trying to make by opposing these common financial products is that we should not count on them for our sole provision in the future. Returns and interest rates on these products usually don't keep up with inflation; asset growth and interest are largely outside of our control. There are great options such as Evangelpreneurism and saving the gravy that people don't even learn about anymore because of the inappropriate dependency on and promotion of the more common financial products.

What about verses like "*And again I say unto you, It is easier for a camel to go through the eye of a needle, than for a rich man to enter into the kingdom of God*" (Matthew 19:24) and "*Jesus said unto him, If thou wilt be perfect, go and sell that thou hast, and give to the poor, and thou shalt have treasure in heaven: and come and follow me*" (Matthew 19:21)?

These are very interesting and often misunderstood parts of Scripture. To understand these verses, we need to back up to at least Matthew 19:16 to learn the context of the verses. When the young man approached the Messiah asking him what he must do to have eternal life, He answers him by saying that he should "enter into life, and keep the commandments." The young man responds that he has been keeping the commandments since youth.

Let's stop for a moment and cover what we have learned from the passage thus far. Here is a man to whom Yeshua gave the answer: to keep the Commandments. The man who said he kept them since his youth seems to be a bit delusional, because no man can be perfect, yet here he claims he is perfect. This is where most people miss the power of what we read.

Jesus knows nobody keeps the law perfectly, hence His mission on earth. He responds to the man by starting with, "If thou wilt be perfect." Wait—Jesus didn't say, "If you will be saved." He said, "If thou wilt be perfect," pointing out that this young man is claiming to be perfect. Jesus transitioned off of salvation to human perfection since it was obvious that the young man was not interested in salvation. When we look up the word in Greek, we see that the word used for "perfect" is not talking about a post life, but is in reference to action. Jesus continues, "If thou wilt be perfect, go and sell that thou hast, and give to the poor, and thou shalt have treasure in Heaven: and come and follow me."

Is Jesus condemning this man's wealth? Of course not. As a matter of fact, He understands it is real and purposeful, and can be used for the poor. Is Jesus calling him out on his sin of being wealthy? Of course not—it is not a sin.

Jesus basically says, "Okay, you think you are sin-free? You are not. You want to be perfect, and you seem a bit egotistical. Okay, I tell you what. Give up the earthly you are hanging on to. Use it by giving it to the poor, but give it up and come put in some hard work."

We then read, "But when the young man heard that saying, he went away sorrowful: for he had great possessions."

Here, we have another example of the man's delusional condition. If he had been perfect in his commandments since his youth, and he understood the God who gave those commandments, he would continue to walk in them and follow Jesus. "You shall have no other gods before me" is one of those commandments, and if the young man was really keeping them like he boasted he was, he would be able to give up the money that he treated as his god and instead follow the One true God.

Basically, in Matthew 19:16-22 we read of Jesus calling out a liar.

Then we have Matthew 19:24, talking about how it is easier for a camel to pass through the eye of a needle than for a rich man to enter into Heaven. If we ignore the fact that the "eye of the needle" may have been referring to a gate in the wall of Jerusalem, which camels had to hunch down to enter, we are still looking at a rich man having a disadvantage. What is Jesus referring to here? This is immediately following what happened with the delusional liar a moment ago who had a love of money. Let me say that again, the young rich man's problem was not that he had money; it was the fact that he had a love of money. His love for money was above his love for God. Jesus is pointing out that rich men (like the one they just dealt with in the passage) have a tendency to love money.

Keep in mind: we end this segment of Scripture with the disciples asking, "Who then can be saved?" (Matthew 19:25).

Jesus responds by saying, "With men this is impossible" (Matthew 19:26). What men is He referring to? Men, all men. So if it is hard for a rich man to get into the Kingdom of Heaven, *it is just as hard* for the poor man to get into Heaven. This obliterates the "anti-rich" argument for anyone who can read.

Jesus doesn't stop there, though; He continues in this verse, after saying that it is impossible for all men to get into Heaven, by saying, "But with Yahweh, all things are possible."

The same thing that saves the poor man is the same thing that saves the rich man, and what is impossible for one is just as impossible for the other.

What this all means is that Matthew 19 encourages us to have our vertical alignment right, with God first. If God is first, being rich or being poor makes no difference to your salvation. Keep in mind that even though we like to focus on the fact that a rich man was told to give up money in order to be a follower, Jesus also tells us we should be just as willing to give up parents, spouses, and children. It is easy to point at the rich man and pretend that the story actually pertains to money. Rarely do we talk about giving up anything else He says we should be willing to give up.

I have to tell you, if we told people that to follow God, it would be necessary to give up the things we have in our lives, fewer people would do it; but when it is something we don't have, like a lot of money, then people don't have a problem. It is easy to give up what you don't actually have.

When we focus on these verses and relate them only to money as opposed to our love and devotion to God, it only reveals we don't understand what we are reading.

I love what you had to say about vertical alignment and, and I see the power that it holds. Is your vertical alignment always identical to your values?

Great question. Many times, people get these things confused, and understandably so. The difference is that values are more along the lines of actions and/or traits that you view as positive. For example, honesty is a value, loyalty is a value, and patience is a value. What you list on your vertical alignment are people, organizations, or areas of life that are important to you.

I would stress again, when it comes to this topic, that I recommend attending our live training or at least getting our digital video course "Meaning of Life."

When you were addressing making your vertical alignment and having your kids do the same, I became a bit anxious, because I have changed what is important in my life recently. After reading your book, I finally have a value system. I feel like a hypocrite if I guide my kids to a vertical alignment, when I know I am guilty of not following the right vertical alignment in the past. How do I help them without being a hypocrite?

This is a huge problem. So many parents think they cannot tell their kids to avoid drugs, sex, drinking, or whatever, because they engaged in these things in the past. Please realize that this is the wrong approach. It does not make you a hypocrite to try to keep your kids from experiencing the pain you have gone through just because you went through it. That is called imparting wisdom, loving, and raising children in the way you want them to go.

It would be hypocritical to tell you to love your children, but to do the loving thing by trying to keep them from making mistakes that harm them. Are you really trying to tell me that if you did crack when you were younger, you wouldn't try to keep your kid from doing it, because you have the wrong definition of "hypocrite"? They could die of an overdose because you didn't want to admit your mistake and let them gain from your wisdom and experience.

Perhaps you may have been a bit promiscuous in your past; even so, you should still tell your kids how important it is to remain pure. You would be the perfect person to tell them how important it is—you may be the only person in their lives who can share with them the pain that sleeping around can cause. A hypocrite is not someone who did something in the past and now tells others they shouldn't do the same thing; that is actually called sharing wisdom. A hypocrite is someone who tells someone not to do something while themselves engaging in that very thing.

Don't feel like you cannot live out, share, and teach vertical alignment because you have done something of which you're not proud. If that were the case, nobody would have a vertical alignment, and the number of problems would just keep growing. The best examples are broken people who turn from their mistakes, place the important things first (mainly God), and live out their proper vertical alignment. The greatest stories are told by the ones who make the unlikeliest comebacks.

Become a hero for your children!

When you talk about living your life as an example and funding events—those that benefit the purpose of spreading the Gospel—do you think they should be done anonymously, or do you think it is okay to have your name attached to the project?

"Take heed that ye do not your alms before men, to be seen of them: otherwise ye have no reward of your Father which is in heaven. Therefore when thou doest thine alms, do not sound a trumpet before thee, as the hypocrites do in the

synagogues and in the streets, that they may have glory of
men. Verily I say unto you, They have their reward.

But when thou doest alms, let not thy left hand know
what thy right hand doeth: That thine alms may be in secret:
and thy Father which seeth in secret himself shall reward
thee openly."—Matthew 6:1–4

This verse is usually referenced when talking about giving (or alms, as Jesus puts it), and there is truth in it. We need to remember, though, that just like the story of the wealthy man who loved his money and didn't want to give it up in order to follow Jesus, it all comes down to the *why*. Why didn't the rich man want to give up his possessions? Because his possessions were the focus of his love; they became the "why" that we discussed earlier.

We notice three words in the first verse that define the meaning of the whole passage: "to be seen." Do not practice righteousness in front of others *to be seen*. Don't give to get recognition; give to give. Just as God and the Messiah did not call on all rich people to give up their wealth (because not all wealthy people love their money), not all people who give do so in order to gain recognition.

If you give for the purpose of promoting yourself, then you should turn your heart over to God (or if by chance you don't believe there is a god, whatever you have on the top of your vertical alignment, assuming that top item is not you) and give anonymously. However, if you give to bring glory to the one you serve, then there is nothing wrong with attaching your name to a donation or project.

For example, let's pretend that Tom Cruise was a Christian and his heart was in the right place. Would it be okay for him to sponsor a 24-hour prayer and help center for battered women, and let the public know? Some would ignorantly say that he should not attach his name on it because of the verse mentioned, and that by attaching his name, he only wants to promote himself. Again, if his heart belongs to God and not a love of self, then this is not the case. By giving money and having his name publically out there, he could encourage others to give. It could make women feel like the center is a safe place to turn, because it now has a measure of credibility. Most importantly, how many millions of people will be inspired to look into Tom's faith because they admire him?

I know that might buck the trend when it comes to what has been taught, but that is because we tend to take teachings out of context, and we need to instead examine Scripture with Scripture, which means we take a look at context, previous passages connecting to the passages we are studying, and original meaning of the words in the earlier language, as well as Scripture elsewhere in the Word that teaches on the same subject to validate findings.

Tom Cruise is actually a great example; look at how many people had the opportunity to explore and embrace

Scientology simply because they saw Tom Cruise prac-
ticing it. Tim Tebow had the same effect; when he wore
Scripture verses under his eyes, millions were invited to
read the Scripture for the first time (and probably many
continue to do so). Because Tim Tebow associated his
public name with his faith, more people were made aware
of that faith.

We see public acts of giving in Scripture, too. In Acts,
Luke (the author) knows that Barnabas sells his land and
gives it all to the cause. How did Luke know? He knew
because Barnabas didn't do it in secret. Instead, he did
it publically enough to not only make Luke aware of the
giving, but also to inspire others to do the same. We see
another example in Acts 5. Ananias and his wife Sappira
sold a possession, and did so without God as their highest priority. They carried out the act in a selfish manner,
and God terminated their existence. Here is the interesting
part, though. Ananias and Sappira didn't have to sell anything! They did it to be seen and to appear to be as devoted
as Barnabas, but God wasn't fooled.

If you are giving or acting financially inside the Body,
then keep it anonymous. This way, it shows no favoritism,
and everyone feels equal in their giving regardless of the
amount. It is not about the amount or being recognized for
the action, but rather as a service to God.

In the general population, I would still recommend
anonymity most of the time, with the exception being if

you can use your influence as an example of Christianity. Then, the focus is on your influence and not your financial success; it just happens to have a financial element to it.

Don't think that this anonymous-versus-known issue only applies to the wealthy. Many times, I have seen people in a church make a show of using big hand motions to bring attention to the fact that they are putting something in the offering plate.

I notice that you sometimes refer to Jesus as Yeshua. Why do you do this?

Yahshua or Yeshua are names that have been gaining more momentum in the Christian faith, as is the name of God: Yahweh, YHVH, and YHWH. Baptists, Methodists, Lutherans, Charismatics, and more are starting to use the Messiah's actual name. Every pastor on earth knows that His name was not Jesus or Iesus, and if we go back to Greek, Aramaic, and Hebrew, this is easily confirmed.

Now, unfortunately, there will be people who think that using His name means that it must be part of a "sacred name movement" thing. Ignorance and pride sometimes motivate people to be closed-minded. I am not saying that if you say "Jesus" you are not talking about the same person, and I'm not saying that you are not saved if you call on Jesus.

"Neither is there salvation in any other: for there is none other name under heaven given among men, whereby we must be saved." —Acts 4:12

If you think about it, the entire Christian faith is a sacred name movement. Since we know His real historical name, we should use it. Even if using another name is fine and permissible, it is not always honoring and loving. If your name is Bob and kids used to call you Sneezy, would you know if they said "Sneezy" they were talking to you? Of course. Would you feel more in a relationship with them if they called you by your actual name when referring to you in prayer and admiration? Absolutely.

Additionally, by using both names interchangeably, I'm trying not to offend those who use either or both.

I was always told that using OPM (Other People's Money) was the smart way to get successful. Homes, cars, boats, and businesses should always be purchased with OPM. You seem against that because of the debt issue, but isn't it worth it?

Using other people's money can work, if by work you mean get you what you want. Have people used it successfully and beat the risk? Sure. My point, though, is it is not the smart thing to do. I know there are people who have robbed a bank and have never been caught; does that mean it is worth the risk? Of course I am not suggesting that using other people's money is akin to robbing a bank; I'm just pointing out that we need to realize the risk—and that is a risk I usually warn against.

I have seen too many people think that because the interest on a car is so low, they will keep the money they saved in the bank and take a loan instead, and just use the interest on the saved money to pay the loan on the car. Then an economic uncertainty happens, the money is gone, and the car is repossessed. They could have owned the car outright with no risk of repossession, but they wanted to use OPM.

What is even worse than people who use OPM for things they could have afforded on their own are people who use OPM to pay for something they could NOT have afforded on their own. This places you in a position of debt AND risk. Even when it comes to mortgages it is preferable to double up payments as a way to get out from under the risk quicker, as well as save tens of thousands of dollars in interest payments. How sad to think if you buy a home for $150,000, you end up paying over $300,000 over the course of a thirty-year mortgage.

I will say, though, that there is a huge difference between personal debt and business debt. If a fairly low-risk debt is taken on in order to produce a lot more money, that is 180 degrees different from taking on personal debt to buy something you want in your life that may not produce much more income.

Your cover seems pretty bold, even possibly offensive. Why did you use such a sensational image?

The answer is actually in the question. Why is making a cross out of money a bad thing, yet having "In God We Trust" on that same money a desired thing? I believe the fact that some people may find the cover shocking just further illustrates the point I'm trying to make—that we have such a misunderstanding of money, and God's approach to it, that we are more offended by an image than we are about record numbers of bankruptcies, foreclosures, and all the other issues we discussed in the book.

One person even asked me if I found it sacrilegious. The answer is absolutely not! If we are to use the money we are given to serve the one true God, then I would say the image is a great reminder to us that we must be good stewards. In a parallel way, those who are not truly serving the Creator of the universe see money as their idol, their god; so for them the image is again appropriate, by pointing out their idolatry. It amazes me how many people literally judged a book by its cover.

The church my husband and I go to asks for pledges for giving. How do we determine our pledge if we are hoping to grow our income over the course of the next year by becoming business owners?

I wouldn't pledge at all if I were you. The idea of taking pledges is a way for churches to plan their budgeting to a certain extent, as well as to get a commitment from members, in hopes they will give more than they would if no pledge was given. While I understand the reasoning, I strongly disagree with the practice.

When we look at Matthew 5:34–36 we are told not to make an oath. There is much discussion on what Yeshua is really talking about and what it means to "swear by Jerusalem," but one verse whose meaning is undeniable is that when it says, "Neither shalt thou swear by thy head, because thou canst not make one hair white or black" (Matthew 5:36), it is talking about making a promise by your own ability. You do not know if you will get laid off four months from now or if the market will dive, taking your pension with it. When you make a pledge you are making a promise before God that you have no control over being able to accomplish.

To take this one step further, making a promise and not being able to keep it is a sin. From my experience, and the experience of church leaders I have spoken with over the past decade, we know that almost half of all pledges to a church are never fulfilled, meaning the very fact that churches ask for them is placing many people in a position where sin enters their life via the churches' efforts to collect money. Not a smart move.

It would be better for churches to concentrate on imparting Biblical teachings regarding making and stewarding money, as this would produce far more revenue and

eliminate the doorway for sin that comes with asking for
pledges.

With only so much money in the economy, don't you think there is a point where not everyone can be successful?

First, in all honesty, most people will not read this book or
start a business, let alone one that is successful. As much
as I wish that were not the case, reality says otherwise. So
no, there is no way that so many people will be successful
that the wealth will run thin.

Beyond that, though, is a much larger misconception:
that there is a finite amount of economic wealth to be had,
and once every part of it is distributed there is no way to
create more. The truth is that there is no cap on the amount
of wealth that can be created! Everyone—yes, everyone—
could be successful. The wealth of an economy is limitless.

Of course this leads to a much larger conversation about
pricing, supply and demand, and such, but the point is
there is more than enough for everyone on the planet to
have control of time and money if we all really decided to.

This limited-resource belief usually leads to another
misconception about money and business: that for one
person to gain, another has to lose. This is simply not true
in a free-enterprise system! As a matter of fact, the opposite is true: When a business owner prospers, his or her
customers prosper in the exchange. If a business doesn't

offer a good service, good product, or good price, the customers will not purchase.

Unfortunately, because many big businesses happen to be in league with big government to eliminate the free-enterprise system, customers have experienced a form of fascism and thought it was free enterprise.

My brother-in-law is a Christian and holds the belief that money is not that important. However, he is not providing for my sister and my nephews. He keeps saying that if the Lord wanted him to have money then He would have given it to him. Is he right? Does the failure really rest on God?

Nope, it is your brother-in-law's responsibility. We know that it is God who gives the power to obtain wealth (Deuteronomy 8:18), and too often believers use this verse to excuse their failings as just an extension of God's will. In reality it is usually a combination of poor Christian teaching on money and laziness.

I am not saying everyone should be or will always be wealthy as far as overflowing with financial riches, but I am saying God commands us to be financially successful to provide for our own families.

Talking about financial matters, the Scriptures tell us:

"But if any provide not for his own, and specially for those of his own house, he hath denied the faith, and is worse than an infidel." —1 Timothy 5:8

Who wants to be worse than an infidel?

Denying your faith by not being a smart earner of money? How is this possible? It is because the author of 1 Timothy knows that the Bible lays out how we are to make money (as does this book), so those who fail to live out the Bible's teaching on this issue are denying what the faith teaches on the issue—which is, they are denying the faith.

Now, let me say, before I get a bunch of hate mail, that there are seasons, tests, trials, and so forth that could put a very Godly man in a position of lack or even poverty, but these are usually temporary and are either caused by sin (gambling, for example) or are from the Father to teach a lesson. These situations are usually easy to discern for they seem to not make logical sense. You may be working hard, you may be doing what has worked before, but for some reason there is no result. This is not what 1 Timothy is referring to. Instead, it is referring to people who are either lazy or engaging in moneymaking activities that are not in line with Biblical free-enterprise teachings.

My husband and I already have a busines; we have hired terrible coaches in the past and can clearly see the difference in you. What help can you offer us? And can you also help our in-laws, who are just getting started but are looking to learn this in a deeper way?

For those who have not yet gotten their feet under them, we offer groups, trainings, and even Certified Business

Operator training, not to mention capital protection services.

For those who have a business and need to have that business succeed, we offer a great suite of services that provide a plug-and-play strategic growth department to any organization.

Visit:

www.JoshTolley.com

www.PurpleMonkeyGarage.com

www.Shyft-Capital.com

Notes

Introduction

1 Employment Benefit Research Institute, *2012 Retirement Confidence Survey—2012 Results*, March 13, 2012, http://www.ebri.org/surveys/rcs/2012/.

2 Charles Swab, "Modern Wealth Survey," May 2019, https://content.schwab.com/web/retail/public/about-schwab/Charles-Schwab-2019-Modern-Wealth-Survey-findings-0519-9JBP.pdf.

3 *Christianity Today International Church Finance and Leadership Journal*, February 2010.

4 Yen, "4 in 5."

5 Tim Reid, "Banks Foreclosing on Churches in Record Numbers," *Reuters*, March 9, 2012, http://www.reuters.com/article/2012/03/09/us-usa-housing-churches-idUSBRE82803120120309.

6 *The Josh Tolley Show*, March 9, 2012.

7 empty tomb, inc., "SCG11 Press Release: In Light of Church Member Giving Declines through 2011, Church Leaders Should Focus on Global Triage Needs Rather than Techniques to Reverse Trends, According to New empty tomb Report," October 11, 2013, http://www.emptytomb.org/scg11pressrel.html.

8 Malachi 3:8, "Will a man rob God? Yet ye have robbed me. But ye say, Wherein have we robbed thee? In tithes and offerings."

Chapter 1

9 Tim Reid, "Church Foreclosures Hit Record in 2011," *Huffington Post Business*, March 8, 2012, http://www.huffingtonpost.com/2012/03/08/church-foreclosures-2011_n_1333655.html.

10   As found in Matthew 6:9–13.

11   Matthew 6:14.

12   Yen, "4 in 5."

13   Jim Forsyth, "More Than Two-Thirds in U.S. Live Paycheck to Paycheck: Survey," *Reuters*, September 19, 2012, http://www. reuters.com/article/2012/09/19/us-usa-survey-paycheck-idUS BRE88I1BE20120919.

14   Naomi Mannino, "Survey: Savings Statistics. Nearly Half Have No Emergency Savings," CreditDonkey, last modified July 3, 2013, http://www.creditdonkey.com/no-emergency-savings.html.

Chapter 2

15   Vivien Su, "Small Town Creates Local Currency to Weather CO-VID-19 Impacts," Pop-Up City, https://popupcity.net/observations/small-town-creates-local-currency-to-weather-covid-19-impacts/.

Chapter 3

16   Pat Hagan, "Stress at Work 'Raises Diabetes Risk by 45%': Strain a Factor Even among the Slim," *Daily Mail*, August 17, 2014, http://www.dailymail.co.uk/health/article-2727447/Stress-work-raises-diabetes-risk-45-Strain-factor-slim.html#ixzz3KaKHeL6V; "Monday Morning Bad for Your Health," *CNN World Business*, February 3, 2005, http://edition.cnn.com/2005/BUSINESS/02/03/monday.pressure/index.html?iref=mpstoryview; Steven Reinberg, "Suicide Now Kills More American's Than Car Crashes," *U.S. News & World Report Health*, September 20, 2012, http://health.usnews.com/health-news/news/articles/2012/09/20/suicide-now-kills-more-americans-than-car-crashes-study; Office of the Assistant Secretary for Planning and Evaluation, "Indicators of Child, Family, and Community Connections: Family, Work, and Child Care," US Department of Health and Human Services, accessed December 4, 2014, http://aspe.hhs.gov/hsp/connections-charts04/ch3.htm.

17   "New Facts on the Increased Cost of Living," *The New York Times*, March 27, 1910, http://query.nytimes.com/mem/archive-free/pdf?res=9807E5D81430E233A25754C2A9659C946196D6CF; Bureau of Labor Statistics, "One Hundred Years of Price Change: The Consumer Price Index and the American Inflation Experience," US Department of Labor, April 2014, http://www.bls.gov/opub/mlr/2014/article/one-hundred-years-of-price-change-the-consumer-price-index-and-the-american-inflation-experience.htm; MeasuringWorth.com calculators, http://www.measuringworth.com.

18   Bureau of Labor Statistics, "Planned Change in the Consumer Price Index Formula April 16, 1998," US Department of Labor, last modified October 16, 2001, http://www.bls.gov/cpi/cpigm02.htm.

19   "Ron Paul 2012 - Inflation Statistics Are Rigged, Bernanke's Money Printing Is a Failure," YouTube video, 9:21, posted by 2012TheRevolution, October 3, 2011, https://www.youtube.com/watch?v=8-3HYVfKQm0.

20   "RON PAUL SLAMMING "CTRL+P" BERNANKE !", YouTube video, 9:11, posted by Zero Point, March 2, 2012, https://www.youtube.com/watch?v=LXAPRi3E-OE.

21   Carmen DeNavas-Walt and Bernadette D. Proctor, "Income and Poverty in the United States: 2013," *Current Population Reports P60-249*, United States Census Bureau, September 2014, http://www.census.gov/content/dam/Census/library/publications/2014/demo/p60-249.pdf.

22   United States Census Bureau, "Median and Average Sales Prices of New Homes Sold in United States," accessed November 21, 2014, https://www.census.gov/construction/nrs/pdf/uspricemon.pdf.

23   United States Census Bureau, *Money Income of Households, Families, and Persons Living in the United States: 1985 (Current Population Reports: Consumer Income, Series P-60, No. 156*, August 1987), http://www2.census.gov/prod2/popscan/p60-156.pdf.

24   "New Residential Sales in October 2014," *U.S. Census Bureau News* (press release), November 26, 2014, http://www.census.gov/construction/nrs/pdf/newressales.pdf.

25   Julie Jacobson, "States with the Most Homes Underwater," *NBC News*, July 26, 2012, http://business.nbcnews.com/_news/2012/07/26/12835769-states-with-the-most-homes-underwater.

Chapter 5

26   Jonathan Owen, "49 Minutes: The Time Each Day the Average Family Spends Together," *The Independent*, May 30, 2010, http://www.independent.co.uk/news/uk/home-news/49-minutes-the-time-each-day-the-average-family-spends-together-1987035.html.

27   Barna Group, "Is Evangelism Going Out of Style?" December 18, 2013, https://www.barna.org/barna-update/faith-spirituality/648-is-evangelism-going-out-of-style#.VHpYM4vF-9V.

28   Ibid.

29   David W. Moore, "Majority of Americans Want to Start Own Business," Gallup, April 12, 2005, http://www.gallup.com/poll/15832/Majority-Americans-Want-Start-Own-Business.aspx.

30   "National Survey Reveals 56 Million Americans Want To Start Their Own Business, But Are Hesitant Due To A Sluggish Economy," *PRWeb*, July 27, 2012 (press release), http://www.prweb.com/releases/2012/7/prweb9739775.htm.

Chapter 7

31   Nicholas Pell, "You Need $2.5 Million to Retire," *Main Street*, June 14, 2014, http://www.mainstreet.com/article/you-need-25-million-retire.

32   Ibid.

33   Walter Updegrave, "Will $4 Million in Retirement Savings Be Enough?" *CNNMoney*, February 2, 2012, http://money-archive.wp.alley.ws/2012/02/02/pf/expert/retirement_saving.moneymag/index.htm.

34   Mandi Woodruff, "A 20-Year-Old Could Need to Save $7 million for Retirement," *Yahoo! Finance*, May 1, 2014, http://finance.yahoo.com/news/a-20-year-old-will-need-to-save--7-million-for-retirement-184050231.html.

35   Sergei Klebnikov, "Personal finance guru Suze Orman says you need at least $10 million to retire early," *Business Insider*, https://www.businessinsider.com/personal-finance/suze-orman-says-you-need-at-least-5-million-to-retire-early-2018-10.

36   Katie Brockman, "Those Earning More Than $100,000 Per Year Are Struggling Financially," *The Motley Fool*, https://www.fool.com/retirement/2020/02/16/report-even-those-earning-more-than-100000-per-yea.aspx.

37   Mark Gongloff, "All the Wealth Accumulated by the Middle Class after 1940 Is Gone," *Huffington Post Business*, October 20, 2014, http://www.huffingtonpost.com/2014/10/20/middle-class-wealth-shrinks-1940s_n_6014874.html.

38   Josh Tolley, "The Practical Poverty Level," *Josh Tolley's Blog*, March 15, 2011, http://joshtolley.wordpress.com/2011/03/15/the-practical-poverty-level.

39   Marcus Harrison Green, "They're raising grandkids with little help, and during a pandemic. Can't we lend them a hand?," *Seattle Times*, https://www.seattletimes.com/seattle-news/theyre-raising-grandkids-with-little-help-and-during-a-pandemic-cant-we-lend-them-a-hand/.

Chapter 9

40　"Alcohol Tests Catch 11 Pilots A Year," WUSA-9, November 12, 2009, http://archive.wusa9.com/news/local/story.aspx?storyid=93593.

41　Greg Botelho and Janet DiGiacomo, "Recall of Nearly 9 Million Pounds of Meat Not Fully Inspected," *CNN*, February 9, 2014, http://www.cnn.com/2014/02/08/us/beef-product-recall/index.html.

42　Brian Palmer, "How Many Kids Are Sexually Abused by Their Teachers?", *Slate*, February 8, 2012, http://www.slate.com/articles/news_and_politics/explainer/2012/02/is_sexual_abuse_in_schools_very_common_.html.

43　Annual Retirement Survey: Wells Fargo/Harris Interactive. Study conducted over a cross section of more than 1,500 middle class Americans between August and September of 2011, published November 16, 2011.

44　Sara Groves appeared on the November 29, 2011, episode of my program.

Chapter 10

45　"Our Founder," J. R. Simplot Company, 2014, http://www.simplot.com/about/our_founder.

Chapter 11

46　CVNutron, "I'm Gay and I Support Chick-Fil-A," *CNN iReport*, August 2, 2012, http://ireport.cnn.com/docs/DOC-823655; Gregory E. Miller, "These Gay New Yorkers Can't Wait for Chick-Fil-A to Hit Their City," *New York Post*, May 7, 2014, http://nypost.com/2014/05/07/nyc-gays-say-ok-to-chick-fil-as-upcoming-expansion.

47　"Hobby Lobby to Open 70 New Stores across the U.S. in 2014," PR Newswire, February 5, 2014, http://www.prnewswire.com/news-releases/hobby-lobby-to-open-70-new-stores-across-the-us-in-2014-243726461.html.

Chapter 12

48　Ernest Passero, "For God, Corps, and Country," *Marine Corps Gazette*, October 1985, accessed November 21, 2014, https://www.mca-marines.org/gazette/god-corps-and-country.

Chapter 14

49 Scott Shane, "Startup Failure Rates—The REAL Numbers," *Small-BizTrends.com*, April 28, 2008, http://smallbiztrends.com/2008/04/startup-failure-rates.html.

50 Simon Ejembi, "Know When Your Small Business Is Failing," *Punch*, May 14, 2013, http://www.punchng.com/business/am-business/know-when-your-small-business-is-failing/.

51 Ben Ryan, "Many U.S. Microbusiness Owners Depend on Second Job," *Gallup*, April 3, 2014, http://www.gallup.com/poll/168215/microbusiness-owners-depend-second-job.aspx.

52 Terry Maxon, "A Reader Asks: Do Airlines Ever Make Money," *Dallas Morning News*, November 16, 2011, http://aviationblog.dallasnews.com/2011/11/a-reader-asks-do-airlines-ever.html.

Chapter 16

53 "Why Are All Wisconsin Car Dealers Closed on Sunday?", CBS Channel 3, February 16, 2010, http://www.channel3000.com/news/Why-Are-All-Wisconsin-Car-Dealers-Closed-Sundays/8323144.

54 Caroline Moss, "My High School No Longer Holds Dances Because Students Would Rather Stay Home And Text Each Other," *Business Insider*, March 10, 2014, http://www.businessinsider.com/high-school-has-no-dances-because-students-stay-home-and-text-2014-2#ixzz3KWQ1CAKG.

55 "Black Friday Report 2012," IBM Digital Analytics Benchmark, November 2012, http://www-01.ibm.com/software/marketing-solutions/benchmark-reports/benchmark-2012-black-friday.pdf.

56 Todd Wasserman, "Mark Cuban's Criticism Aside, Facebook Page Conspiracy Claim Is No Slam Dunk," *Mashable*, November 15, 2012, http://mashable.com/2012/11/15/facebook-conspiring-marketers-to-buy-ads.

57 Social@Ogilvy, "Facebook Zero: Considering Life after the Demise of Organic Reach," March 6, 2014, http://social.ogilvy.com/facebook-zero-considering-life-after-the-demise-of-organic-reach/.

58 Siim Sainas, "Influencer with 2.6M Followers Failed to Sell 36 T-Shirts," *Medium*, https://medium.com/@siimulation/influencer-with-2-6m-followers-failed-to-sell-36-t-shirts-2f72e0d408a1.

59 Zach Miners, "Why More Businesses Are Unfriending Facebook," *PCWorld*, April 10, 2014, http://www.pcworld.com/article/2142420/how-marketers-lost-faith-in-facebook.html.

Chapter 17

60 Family Business Institute, "Succession Planning," accessed December 4, 2014, http://www.familybusinessinstitute.com/index.php/ Succession-Planning.

Chapter 18

61 Ali Meyer, "New Record: Federal Tax Revenues Top $3T for 1st Time," *CNSNews.com*, October 15, 2014, http://cnsnews.com/news/ article/ali-meyer/new-record-federal-tax-revenues-top-3t-1st-time.

62 Chris Isidore, "America's Lost Trillions," *CNNMoney*, June 9, 2011, http://money.cnn.com/2011/06/09/news/economy/household_ wealth/index.htm.

63 Peter S. Goodman, "Europe Is Probably in Recession. Can Its Leaders Move Fast and Deliver Relief?" *The New York Times*, March 9, 2020, https://www.nytimes.com/2020/03/09/business/ europe-recession-coronavirus.html; Yen Nee Lee, "Hong Kong announces over $15 billion budget to lift economy out of recession," *CNBC*, February 23, 2021, https://www.cnbc.com/2021/02/24/ hong-kong-announces-budget-to-lift-economy-out-of-covid-recession.html; Peter S. Goodman, "Why the Global Recession Could Last a Long Time," *The New York Times*, April 1, 2020, https://www. nytimes.com/2020/04/01/business/economy/coronavirus-recession. html.

64 Noah Rayman, "U.S. Millionaires Club Grows to Almost Ten Million," *Time*, March 13, 2014, http://time.com/23764/u-s-millionaires-club-grows-to-almost-10-million.

65 Darina Lynkova, "27 Millionaire Statistics: What percentage of Americans are millionaires?" *SpendMeNot*, February 5, 2021, https://spendmenot.com/blog/what-percentage-of-americans-are-millionaires/#:~:text=The%20Global%20Wealth%20Report%20 says,with%20the%20most%20millionaire%20list.

66 Lyn Riddle, "Ex-Teacher Lives Modest Life, Leaves $8.4 Million Gift," *USA Today*, January 30, 2014, http://www.usatoday.com/story/news/ nation/2014/01/30/millionaire-teacher-gift/5065425.

67 Aixa Velez, "Secret Millionaire Gives Fortune to Alma Mater," *NBCNews*, March 5, 2010, http://www.nbcnews.com/id/35729174/ ns/us_news-giving/t/secret-millionaire-gives-fortune-alma-mater/#. VHtKlYvF-9U.

Chapter 19

68 Kevin Clarke, "Collateral Damage: Microloans Gone Bad," *U.S. Catholic* 76, no. 3 (March 2011): 39, http://www.uscatholic.org/culture/social-justice/2011/02/collatoral-damage-microloans-gone-bad.

69 Maria Cohut, "Financial Hardship Is a Top Risk Factor for Suicide Attempt," *Medical News Today*, September 8, 2020, https://www.medicalnewstoday.com/articles/financial-hardship-is-a-top-risk-factor-for-suicide-attempts.

FAQs

70 Matt Flegenheimer, "$1 Million Medallions Stifling the Dreams of Cabdrivers," *The New York Times*, November 14, 2013, http://www.nytimes.com/2013/11/15/nyregion/1-million-medallions-stifling-the-dreams-of-cabdrivers.html?_r=0.

About the Author

JOSH TOLLEY is a nationally syndicated talk-show host with listeners in all fifty states, as well as 160 nations. He is a Liberty Award nominee, was featured in the short film *Elektable*, and even served as a national television anchor for the Free and Equal Elections Foundation presidential debate in October 2012. He has appeared on CBS, NBC, TBN, Messianic.TV, the Church Channel, Al Jazeera, and many other television and radio shows around the world.

His business and strategy training has been heard by hundreds of thousands of people around the planet, and the change it has brought not only to businesses but to lives is palpable. His bold stance on faith and his use of logic, reason, and strategy have led people to truth and have even saved lives by giving hope to the hopeless.

For information on training, online courses,
or speaking events, go to:

www.JoshTolley.com

www.EvangelpreneurBook.com